PRASE FOR *A Paperboy's Fable*

"*A Paperboy's Fable* is a great book for entrepreneurs of all ages. It is a fun read and packed with valuable insights."
— **Derek Lidow**, Global CEO, Professor at Princeton University and author of Startup Leadership

"What Deep Patel has to say, on the basis of his research, interviews and reflections, is a true inspiration for millennials—and well worth pondering."
— **The Huffington Post**

"Prescient and insightful well beyond his years, Deep Patel provides a delightful account of entrepreneurship and the ingredients for success. Budding entrepreneurs and experienced veterans alike will learn and be inspired from the story of Ty Chandler and the lessons embedded therein."
— **William Kerr**, Professor at Harvard Business School and faculty chair of the Launching New Ventures program for executive education

"I was rooting for Ty Chandler as he made his way from opportunity to success. The bonus is a set of lessons for every entrepreneur."
— **Sanjay Parthasarathy**, technology expert and former executive at Microsoft; CEO of Indix

"*A Paperboy's Fable* epitomizes Warren Buffett's investment philosophy."
— **Seeking Alpha**

"This straightforward yet insightful book will shoot directly from Mr. Patel's heart and into yours. At once a solid business book and inspirational fairytale, it could be read by anyone interested in entrepreneurship, self-help and personal growth."
— **MeiMei Fox**, *New York Times* bestselling author

"Deep is wise beyond his years! *A Paperboy's Fable* is a hidden gem full of rich entrepreneurial insight that only somebody like Deep could tell in an enjoyable and educational format. I highly recommend this book to anybody with the entrepreneurial 'itch!'"
— **Jeff Boss**, *Forbes* and *Entrepreneur* contributor, author of *Navigating Chaos* and former Navy SEAL

A
PAPERBOY'S
FABLE

THE **11** PRINCIPLES OF SUCCESS

DEEP PATEL

A POST HILL PRESS BOOK
ISBN: 978-1-68261-004-6
ISBN (eBook): 978-1-68261-005-3

A PAPERBOY'S FABLE
The 11 Principles of Success
© 2016 by Deep K. Patel
All Rights Reserved

Cover Design by Quincy Alivio

The information in this book constitutes the author's opinions. Due to the rate at which conditions change, the author reserves the right to alter and update his opinions at any time. While every attempt has been made to verify the information in this book, the author does not assume any responsibility for errors, inaccuracies, or omissions.

Post Hill Press
275 Madison Avenue, 14th Floor
New York, NY 10016
posthillpress.com

Ty Chandler needs a job.

It's the beginning of his senior year in high school, and if he wants to save up for things like gas for his car, going to movies, and senior prom — to say nothing of college — he needs to start fast. All the regular jobs — bag boy, movie usher, and landscaper — are taken, but one day during his morning jog before school, Ty hears the local paperboy grumbling on his cell phone about quitting.

He asks the paperboy how much he makes each week.

"Diddly," says the paperboy (who is actually a grown man). "Nobody reads the paper anymore. It's a dying market."

But Ty looks up and down his own street, then the three surrounding streets, and he smiles. "Then it's ripe for opportunity," he says confidently. "If you're quitting, can I have the job?"

Ty gets the job and takes over the old paperboy's route, which consists of just nine houses spread over three measly streets. But, he has ambitions over the whole territory, which includes a total of seven streets and more than two hundred homes.

Ty's goal is to make enough money to live the lifestyle he chooses. He achieves his goal — and then some — in record time by applying the Eleven Principles of Success, revealed below.

TABLE OF CONTENTS

INTRODUCTION

Why a Paperboy?

"It was a bizarre, unforgettable experience," my father said, recalling his experiences as a paperboy in Boston when he was my age — just sixteen years old. "The papers were heavy and mornings were chilly. I often rode on slippery, snow-streaked roads, and to top it off I made less than minimum wage." To deliver his newspapers, he rode a rusty blue bike, held together by a few decaying bolts.

My grandfather, a native of India, had immigrated to Kenya to look for employment, and shortly afterward, met my grandmother. They married and within a year, my father was born. Following their return to India, and after years of excruciating work, my grandfather, my grandmother, my father, and my uncle moved to Boston. Inspired by my grandfather's example of perseverance, my father took a job as a paperboy, where he learned many essentials of business that he still carries with him today. Soon they made enough money to purchase a small, rundown dry cleaner. My dad jokingly said he preferred working at the dry cleaner since his hands wouldn't be inked black at the end of the day. In reality, however, a family-owned dry cleaner run by three people was just as wearying, especially while two of them were enrolled in college and attempting to learn a new language.

After meeting my mom, their final journey was to Macon, Georgia, my birthplace, where they purchased a hotel with the money they had earned from the dry-cleaning business. Working at the hotel and running a small real estate business on the side was strenuous. However, it taught them many important elements of success that they now use to make life easier for their respective families.

I am a sixteen-year-old student with a keen interest in exploring the backbone of American business and economic growth. I was looking for a tale that weaved in universal business truths in entertaining, informative nuggets, and realized that my father's story was precisely what I was looking for. So I wrote it down.

A Paperboy's Fable tells the story of a teenager's rise as a small-business owner. By becoming a paperboy, our hero chooses one of the least growth-centric professions around and makes a mint. He achieves his success by focusing on eleven critical areas of business, including recognizing opportunity, harnessing ingenuity, overcoming objections, customer service, creating raving fans, and crushing it with consistency.

After I finished the tale, the responses from readers were amazing, and I realized that the story might resonate with people beyond my circle of friends and family.

In order to ground the book with real-life examples, I approached a handful of people — executives, entrepreneurs, business school professors, and business gurus — and asked if they'd be willing to talk about the sparks in their careers. The book concludes with interviews from these fifteen extraordinary people, offering insights into their careers, as well as advice to aspiring entrepreneurs.

"I was a paperboy for two and a half years in Cornwall-on-Hudson, where I grew up. I delivered a morning paper from about the time I was eleven till I was thirteen. It was a tremendous learning experience. You had to be disciplined and you had to get up early. I had to be up by 5:30 a.m. and had to have all the newspapers on doorsteps by 6:30 a.m. I had a two-and-a-half-mile route, and this was fifty miles north of New York City, where the winters can be quite bracing. You have to interact with your customers and exercise salesmanship to get new customers. You need interpersonal relationships as you collect the subscription money. You have an occasional opportunity to deal with dogs who are off leash. I learned a lot from it."

General David Petraeus,
former director of the CIA

THE FIRST PRINCIPLE OF SUCCESS:

Recognizing Opportunity

Ty Chandler bolted past the sleepy streets of his subdivision, looping around the little park with its tiny gazebo and walking trails that linked together the seven streets of Hampton Squares. He'd run junior varsity and varsity track until last year, when he decided to focus on his studies and apply to the top five schools on his dream list of colleges.

With his senior year about to start, Ty had only a few months left to make a good impression on admission boards at Ivy League schools. No wonder he was up before the dawn, running wind sprints through the sleepy streets of Sunnydale, Georgia.

Ty made his last mad dash around the park and then, crouching, he paused to catch his breath. After standing to stretch his arms, he admired the bucolic setting before him: tree-lined streets of darkened houses full of working folks like his parents and retirees like his next-door neighbors.

It had been a good place to grow up — playing stickball in the street, learning how to ride his bike on the wide sidewalks, enjoying picnics in the park, and experiencing his first kiss in the gazebo. But now it was time to say goodbye to his childhood and focus on his immediate challenge: getting into an A-list school and starting the next chapter of his life, as a college freshman.

The task was close at hand and, beyond polishing his academic résumé with a senior year's worth of perfect attendance, maintaining his 4.0 GPA, and adding a roster of extracurricular activities to his schedule, Ty needed money for college. That meant a new job.

He'd worked all summer at the movie theater downtown, tearing tickets and serving up popcorn and soda; once school was in session, though, his manager had let go of half the staff, including Ty. He'd been applying for part-time jobs all over town ever since, but Ty had gotten a late start. All the usual spots — busboy, waiter, grocery-store bagger, and cashier — were already taken.

As Ty rounded Summer Street for the brief walk home, he heard a strange voice grumbling on a cell phone, and saw a man standing beneath a streetlight. In front of him was a stack of folded papers, and beside that a crumpled messenger bag that read "Sunnydale Sentinel."

"I'm over it," the man was saying into his phone. "After this week, they're gonna have to find a new paperboy. Hey, I'll call you later. Let me unload these last papers and then I'll be done for the morning."

After the man hung up, Ty approached him. "Excuse me," he said.

The man jumped. He was in his mid-forties, about the same age as Ty's dad, and was lean and wiry, with curly hair under a battered *Sunnydale Sentinel* cap. "Geez, kid, you startled me," he said.

"Sorry," Ty said, stepping into the light cast by the streetlight. "I couldn't help but overhear that you might be…quitting?"

"Not *might*," the man said. "This here is my official last week." He looked up at Ty as if for the first time. With a grin he asked, "Why, you interested?"

"Maybe," Ty said. "What's it pay?"

"Diddly," the man grunted, beginning to shove the newspapers into his delivery bag. "And getting worse every week."

"Define *diddly*," Ty said.

"Each house pays six dollars per week," the man said. "I get to keep half of that."

Tyler frowned. The man had already filled his bag with what looked to be fewer than a dozen papers. "Is that all you're delivering today?"

"Yup," the man said, standing and sliding the bag over his shoulder. "My territory's all of the Hampton Squares subdivision, but less than a dozen houses still subscribe to the paper."

Ty did the math: the paperboy was going to make only thirty-six dollars that week. No wonder he was quitting! Ty made that in one shift at the movie theater and got to watch free movies to boot.

"But there are seven whole streets in this subdivision!" said Ty.

The man chuckled. "Yup, over two hundred homes. But kid, it's the *newspaper*."

"So?"

The man laughed. "When's the last time *you* read the newspaper?"

Ty wrinkled his nose. That was like being asked when was the last time he used a payphone. "What…offline?"

The man laughed. "My point exactly. Nobody reads the paper anymore, kid. It's a dying market."

Ty shook his head, looking up and down his street, and then at the three streets on either side. Over two hundred homes, and each one a blank slate. If he could sell them all a subscription to the *Sunnydale Sentinel*, that would be $600 a week.

That was nearly three times what he'd made at the theater. Ty realized that the outgoing paperboy was thinking only of the bottom line — and therefore missing bigger opportunities and possibilities.

"Then it's ripe for opportunity," he said, thrusting out his chin. "If you're really quitting, can I have the job?"

"Sure, kid. Meet me here tomorrow morning, same time, and hand me your résumé. I'll turn it in and we'll see what happens. But between you and me, it's yours to lose."

"What's that mean?"

"The *Sentinel's* practically begging for paperboys," he confided as he got into his battered station wagon at the curb. "They'll probably hire you before I'm even done."

"Is that gonna be a problem?" Ty asked.

"Be doing me a favor, kid," the man said with a weary wave before driving off into the dark.

Ty stared after the departing lights, tingling with anticipation. What Ty hadn't told the man was that, unlike him, he'd grown up in Hampton

Squares. Sure, it was a series of sleepy streets, but that was in his favor. Half the folks in the subdivision were retirees. They could be spending their long days reading the newspaper in a leisurely manner, on their front porches or back decks, in their living rooms or breakfast nooks.

Inside the paper was everything they needed to make the most of their retirement: stories about distant destinations in the Leisure section, movie reviews in Arts & Entertainment, and dozens of volunteer opportunities listed each week in the Local section.

The other residents were working-class folks, like his mom. But even so, there were things the paper had that they needed as well: weekly deals on new cars, want ads if they were looking for a new job, and classified ads for replacement dishwashers or handymen if their sinks were leaking.

The old paperboy had assured Ty this was a dying business. That's probably how he sold the papers as well. Ty could practically see the poor guy shuffling from door to door. His big pitch was probably: "You don't really want a newspaper, do you?" All Ty had to do — if he got the job — was convince his customers that the paper represented an *opportunity*, and how much *value* they could get for six bucks a week. These days, that was less than a daily cup of coffee!

Considering his desire to make as much money as he possibly could before heading off to college, and the lack of jobs for kids his age during the school year, it was pretty much his only option.

Ty had no choice but to become a paperboy — and the best darn paperboy Hampton Squares had ever seen. Now all he had to do was figure out what the heck a résumé was by the tomorrow morning…

"I went to India in 1996, and I saw it was ready to move into a software space. At MIT I wrote an op-ed piece about how India could be a software superpower, and that was in 1989. I realized this was an opportunity — Bill going there; he had never been there. And this was an opportunity to make a couple points: that there was a market for Microsoft software outside of Europe and the US and Japan, and Bill got to see that. But even more importantly, Microsoft has always been a platform company, and developers on platform have always been super important. Having Bill there, he got it, he got the energy and enthusiasm, and a direct result of that was heading up a software-development center. So both at the market and supply level, as part of the supply chain for software, I think the bells went off. It was the right timing. When 1997 happened, there was an incredible amount of interest, and every politician was talking about this in their speeches. Then the year 2000 bug was on the horizon, and people realized the only way to deal with it was to have a software company help them out. It was a good storm, if you will."

Sanjay Parthasarathy,
CEO of Indix

THE SECOND PRINCIPLE OF SUCCESS:
Investing in Success

T y rode his bike home from the *Sunnydale Sentinel* headquarters, beaming with pride. It wasn't so much from the freshly signed contract in his backpack, or even the fact that he could start his new route the next morning. It was from all the ideas buzzing around in his head!

As he rode through downtown Sunnydale, he could feel the change in the air. One season was ending and another beginning — summer passing the baton to fall. The storefronts and display windows had changed their themes from the red, white, and blue of July to the golden colors of autumn.

His first stop of the day, Sunnydale Savings and Loan, was bustling at this hour, and Ty had to remind himself that it was never summer vacation for local businesses, least of all for the town's one and only bank.

"Hi, Ty," said Carol, the teller who had helped him set up his savings account at the beginning of that summer. "What can we do for you today?"

"Hi, Carol," he said. "I'd like to check on my savings account and withdraw some money."

Carol wagged a finger playfully. "You're going in the wrong direction, Ty. You're supposed to be depositing money, not withdrawing it, remember?"

"But what if it's for an investment?" he asked as he watched her enter his account information on her computer.

"A little young to be playing the stock market, aren't you?" Carol said as she printed out his balance for him.

"It's more...it's more like an investment in myself," Ty said slowly, as if only just now realizing it himself. He looked down at the paper she had handed him. He had $1,200 in savings, thanks to his summer job at the Sunnydale Cinema. He'd wanted to save up enough for a car for his senior year, but then he realized that, with all his activities along with having to keep up his grades, he wouldn't have much free time to drive around anyway. That had allowed him to put a significant chunk of his weekly paycheck into his savings account.

Still, he didn't want to raid his account too heavily. He was hoping to get an academic scholarship to one of his top five schools, but even then he knew there would be living expenses like furnishing his dorm, entertainment, transportation, and the like. He didn't want to have to ask his mom for stuff like that, so he was trying to save at least $5,000 for incidentals during his freshman year. Not a ton, but the most reasonable figure he could come up with given his new job prospects.

"Can I withdraw one hundred dollars?" he asked, filling out a withdrawal slip and sliding it beneath the window.

"You can withdraw anything you want," Carol said. "Especially if it's an investment in yourself." She winked, processed the slip, and handed him five twenty-dollar bills.

Ty held up his bills and winked back. "What if I told you I could turn each of these into a hundred dollars?" he teased.

"I'd tell you to come and apply for a job here at the bank, because we need that kind of financial aptitude!"

Ty took his crisp twenty-dollar bills and went straight to the bike shop around the corner.

"How can I help you, young man?" asked Giuseppe, the shop owner.

"I just got a job delivering papers around my neighborhood," Ty explained.

Giuseppe scratched the balding head beneath his "Gears by Giuseppe" baseball cap. "They still deliver papers?" he asked. "By hand?"

"Well, by bike anyway," Ty said. "That's why I'm here. My bike's in pretty good shape, but I know I'm going to be using it a lot this school year so could you just check it out — kick the tires, give it a tune-up, and make it really fly?"

"Sure thing, kid," the old man said. "You want Giuseppe's 'Back to School' special."

"How much does that run?" Ty asked.

Giuseppe peered back at him, scratching his stubbly chin. "You start your job yet?"

"Tomorrow morning," Ty said. "So if there's a coupon or anything…"

Giuseppe grinned. "How's seventy bucks, out the door, top to bottom rehab?"

Ty frowned. He wasn't a great negotiator, but at this point every twenty-dollar bill counted. He didn't want to go over his budget on his first day in business! "Can we make it sixty?" he asked.

Giuseppe narrowed his eyes. "That's a tall order, kid. I'm not so sure about that."

Ty thought for a minute, and then smiled. "I got a free newspaper subscription for my family for being a paperboy," he said. "But my mom already reads it online. I have to pass by here on my way to school every morning, so…I could throw in a free paper every weekday if we can agree on sixty bucks."

"Deal!" Giuseppe said, shaking Ty's hand. "I like the way you think, kid. But I like the way you pay better," he added when Ty slid him three crisp twenty-dollar bills. "I close at five, so if you want to come back then, I'll have your bike ready."

Ty nodded and walked back out onto the street. He looked down at his list and strolled down to the Discount Drug Store. Along with his contract, the paper had given him the names and addresses of his ten current customers. Ty thought it might be a nice touch to give each one a greeting card with a personal handwritten note inside. It would be his way of saying, "Thanks for being a loyal customer."

As he stood in front of the greeting-card aisle a college-age girl came over. "Hi, I'm Chelsea. How can I help you today?"

Ty blushed; she was pretty. "Well, I'm starting a new job tomorrow," he explained, "and I want to give my customers a greeting card, you know, to start off on the right foot. But these" — he held out a flowery card that would be just perfect for his neighbor, Mrs. Worsham — "are five bucks each!"

Chelsea nodded. "Yes, they've gone up in the past few years. How many customers do you have?"

"I have ten now," he said, "but I hope to have more by next week, and many more the week after that. But by then I'll be making a profit so I can afford more. Do you have anything just as nice but a little —" Ty stopped, embarrassed.

"Cheaper?" she asked. "Sure. We have a whole line of ninety-nine-cent cards over there, so you could get ten of those for the price of just two of the fancier cards."

Ty looked at a few, but they weren't quite as nice. Chelsea saw the look on his face and smiled. "Or," she said, picking up a box at the end of the aisle, "we have bulk greeting cards."

"What are those?" Ty asked. He'd never heard of bulk cards. Then again, aside from his mom's birthday card every year, he wasn't a big greeting-card shopper.

"They've got twelve greeting cards inside, with different pictures on the cover like flowers or an old Victorian house or puppies."

He looked at the box, warming to the idea. "What do they say inside?" he wondered.

"What do you want it to say?" she said.

"Greetings from your new paperboy!"

"What's that?" she asked, crumpling her nose.

"You know, the guy who delivers your papers every morning."

"I know what it is," she laughed. "I just…do they still have those?" When he frowned at her she said, "Sorry, bad joke. But no, I don't think we have that. These ones are blank, though," she said, handing him a different box. "And look, the cards show a variety of styles of old-fashioned cottages. On the inside you could write: 'Where would you like me to throw your paper each morning?'"

"I might do that," he said, reaching for another box. "And for potential customers, I could say, 'Imagine your own paper on your front stoop every morning.'"

"I like that," she said as she accompanied him to the cash register. Ty was happy because he'd saved himself a lot of money, which he could now invest in some other way to make his customers love him. Along the way to the cash register, he saw a sign for passport photos.

"Do you do the passport photos here?" he asked.

She paused halfway to the counter. "Yeah, why?"

"How much are they?" he asked.

"Two dollars a print."

"Could I get ten, like...today?"

She smiled. "Sure. I can print them up in about five minutes. Is that soon enough?"

"Perfect," he said. He stood in front of a green screen as Chelsea pointed a camera at him.

"Smile!" she said, and he did. After all, he was investing in himself. Why wouldn't he smile?

"He and I and John Dvorak and some other computer people in Silicon Valley all sat down and founded CNET. The original idea was not to do a website; it was to do a television network. It was supposed to be the Computer Network. That didn't work out; they couldn't raise any money for that, and I couldn't help them. So they just decided: we'll do a website, and that ended up being what we did."

Gina Smith,
award-winning tech journalist

THE THIRD PRINCIPLE OF SUCCESS:
Harnessing Ingenuity

Ty was grateful that he'd started delivering papers the week before school started. This gave him all day, rather than just the mornings and evenings, to get used to his new job and excel at it.

He started bright and early Monday morning, with a fresh stack of newspapers that had been delivered to his doorstep at 5 a.m. The scent of newsprint and copper, warm and fragrant, filled the air as he rolled his customers' papers. Because the weather forecast predicted a morning shower, he slid each paper into one of the flimsy clear-plastic bags provided by the *Sunnydale Sentinel*.

He was glad the publisher provided a few extra copies because he ripped half of them in his eagerness to fold and stuff the papers quickly. And he ripped a few more when he tried to put his greeting cards inside. They bent in an unflattering way, and obscured the front page of the newspaper but, by trial and error, Ty realized that if he slid them inside the already-folded papers, they held their shape better and wouldn't be curled when the subscribers opened them.

By 5:30 he was on the road, his newly tuned-up bicycle cruising through the silent streets. He knew the houses well and, since it was early and none of the lights were on, he could practice tossing the papers onto the porches so that they fell just right, centered on the welcome mat.

He was going to get off his bike at each house and place the papers carefully onto the mats but he knew he wouldn't have time for such luxuries once he'd doubled, tripled, even quadrupled his customer load.

With so few customers the route was done quickly, and by six Ty was back at his house, contemplating the half-dozen extra copies the newspaper had delivered. He set aside one for Giuseppe, the friendly bike-shop owner, and still had five left over.

Inspired, he slipped quietly into the house — his mom was still asleep — and dashed to his room. The paper had given him a printout of every house in his district, all seven streets of the Hampton Squares subdivision.

The nine houses that were already customers had been printed in red. Houses that had been customers at one time but failed to renew their subscriptions were printed in green, and houses that had never signed up for the paper were printed in black.

Ty made a quick tally. He had nine current customers printed in red, twenty-one former customers printed in green and 177 customers printed in black. He figured out that if he wanted to sign up every house in his territory, he had 198 opportunities to do so.

If, instead of just throwing away or recycling his five extra papers every day, he rolled them and put each in a bag with a welcome note, card, or message from their "potential new paperboy," he might not only win back those twenty-one former customers, but also entice those 177 households that had never subscribed in the first place.

At five free papers a week, it would take him thirty-five weeks to hit all the houses. At that rate, it would take him most of the fall semester to hit every house with a free paper and welcome note, but it was better than nothing and would count toward his yearlong goal of signing up every single household on his route.

For now, he took five of the leftover greeting cards he'd gotten at the drug store and wrote the following message:

Hello, and please enjoy this complimentary copy of the Sunnydale Sentinel. My name is Ty Chandler and I am your local paperboy. Please call or text me at 478-393-3417 if you'd enjoy getting the paper like this every morning. Happy reading! —Ty

Once they were sealed together with five of his leftover passport photos, Ty got back on his bike to hit the first five addresses on his prospect list of lapsed customers.

Once those were delivered, he set about doing his usual chores — mowing the lawn, cleaning his room, registering for classes online, scouting colleges — until early afternoon. Then he freshened up, put on his best smile, and went out to greet his customers.

His first house was Ms. Brubaker's, three houses down. She answered on the second knock, eager and spry despite being in her early eighties. "Can I help you, young man?" she asked, peering at him through her screen door.

"Yes, ma'am," he said. "I'm Ty, your new paperboy. I just wanted to come around and introduce myself."

"You're not selling anything, are you?" she asked cautiously.

"Nope, just making sure everything went okay with your delivery this morning."

She smiled. "Now I recognize you," she said, inching through the screen door to join him on the porch. She wore a faded blue housedress and pink slippers, and smelled like lilacs. "You put your picture in my paper!"

"That's so you know who to come looking for if something goes wrong," he teased.

She arched one wispy white eyebrow and frowned. "Now that you mention it," she said, pointing toward her lawn. "The sprinklers went off again before I had a chance to pick up my paper. It got all wet."

"But it was in a plastic bag," he said. His first day — his first house, even — and he already had a complaint?

"That cheap stuff?" she harrumphed. "I've called the paper and complained a dozen times over the years. They don't care."

"Well, I do," he said. "I care very much. It's my first day on the job, and I want all my customers to be happy. What? Why are you looking at me like that?"

"You sure you aren't selling something, boy?" Ms. Brubaker asked, eyeing him.

"No, ma'am," he said. "I'm just very grateful to you for being a customer and want to make sure you're happy." He looked around the porch, the floorboards warped and covered with leaves. "Is there anywhere I can toss the paper where it *won't* get wet?"

"Not really," she said, shaking her head. "Every morning the sprinklers get my whole porch wet."

He walked down the porch steps and spotted the problem right away. "Well, here," he said, turning over the hose. "You had your sprinkler pointing in the wrong direction."

He made sure the attachment was facing the yard and not the porch, and turned on the hose manually. It sprayed the dry yard with a stream of six clear jets that reached nearly to the sidewalk. He turned off the hose. "Now when the timer comes on tomorrow," he explained, "your lawn will get wet, but your paper won't."

"Thank you, young man," she said, suddenly beaming. "I've been meaning to do that for weeks!"

With a wave goodbye, Ty headed to the next house.

While everyone was nice, and even pleasantly surprised that he'd made a personal call to their home, most had complaints about the previous delivery man.

"His car would wake me up every morning at five thirty," said Mr. Johnson.

"Well, I have a bike," Ty told him. "So that won't be a problem anymore."

"There was a tear in the plastic bag this morning," complained Mrs. Evans, "and the dew got the paper wet. I couldn't read half of the front page."

"I'm afraid that's my fault," he said, blushing slightly. "It's my first day, so I was overeager and might have shoved your paper in too fast!"

"No," she explained, letting him off the hook. "It's happened before. Those clear plastic bags are just cheap!"

Ty had to agree, and after he'd met his last customer of the day he took a quick trip downtown to see if he could rectify the situation. The sun was nearly setting as he strolled into Harper's Hardware Store, where

Mr. Harper himself greeted him in a booming voice. He was a rotund, middle-aged man in a bright-red work apron.

"Welcome to Harper's, young man. How can I help you today?"

"I'm not sure," Ty confessed. "I'm a paperboy. The plastic bags the paper gives me have been ripping and my customers are complaining. I thought you might have something of better quality."

Mr. Harper narrowed his eyes and scratched his chin. "What an odd request," he said, slapping Ty on the shoulder and guiding him toward a nearby aisle. "It's not often a customer stumps me right off the bat, but I have to admit no one's ever asked me anything like that before."

"I just assumed the paper would have better bags," Ty grumbled.

"Now that you mention it," Mr. Harper said, "half the mornings my own paper was damp!"

"Do you live in Hampton Squares subdivision?" Ty asked. "If you do, this will help you, too."

"Unfortunately, no," Mr. Harper said. "And I stopped getting the paper years ago. Now, here we have the storage-bag section. I'm not sure if any of these will be up your alley, but we can look."

They started looking over the heavy-duty plastic bags, but they were too big, too small, too oddly sized or too bulky for his purposes. And all were far too expensive!

"Do they all cost this much?" Ty asked.

"Unfortunately, yes," said Mr. Harper. "Plastic storage is big business. Now, over here…"

But Ty stopped him. "What are these?" he asked, noticing several racks of thin red bags.

"Those?" Mr. Harper said, wrinkling his nose. "Those are umbrella bags. Stores buy them in bulk and put them by the front doors when it's raining so customers can stow their umbrellas without dripping all over the store."

"They're long," Ty said, "but about the right size for a newspaper."

"Not for the Sunday paper," Mr. Harper said, joining Ty next to the display. "That sucker's big."

Ty nodded. "I think the paper uses a different bag on Sundays."

"You're right," said Mr. Harper. "So you're only on the hook for six soggy days a week."

"Not with your help," Ty said, fingering the red plastic.

It was thin, but more durable than his current bags. Not only that, but the color would be easier to see for his older customers, particularly on those days Ty might be off his game and lob their papers into the bushes.

"Here," said Mr. Harper as he reached for the display rack. "These bags are for those purse-size umbrellas, so they might be a better fit for the paper."

Ty nodded, taking the stack of plastic bags from his hand. "I'd have to roll them tighter," he murmured, "but these could work. Can I ask how much?"

Mr. Harper led them to the cash register. "They're $7.24 per box of five hundred," he said.

Ty nodded, doing the mental math.

"It sounds like a lot of wrappers," Mr. Harper said, "but if you're tossing out 100 papers every morning...well, is it going to be worth it to you?"

Ty nodded. "It's something I want to do right now," he said. "It's worth it to me to make my customers happy, especially just starting out."

Mr. Harper nodded. "Sure. Sure, kid, but—"

"Ty," he said, sticking out his hand.

Mr. Harper shook his hand. "Ty, sure thing." He looked down at his own nametag, which read only "Mr. Harper." "I'm assuming you know who I am."

"Why do you think I came straight to you?" Ty said with a smile.

"Well, listen, Ty, you can't start your customers on nice, thick, solid red bags that never get their papers wet, then let them down two weeks from now when the box runs out and you don't have it in your budget to replace them."

Ty nodded. "You're right," he said. "I'd have to buy them every few weeks."

"So is it worth it, Ty?" asked Mr. Harper.

Ty frowned. "Not at that price," he admitted. "Is there a way to get it down any?"

Mr. Harper chuckled. "Well, I give discounts to local entrepreneurs," he said. "And you certainly qualify for that, so…" His voice trailed off as he fiddled with a calculator. "That brings you down to six bucks a box. Better, right?"

Ty nodded, still biting his lower lip. "I'm looking for five bucks a box," he confessed, remembering Mr. Giuseppe at the bike shop. "Listen, I have to deliver a paper at the bike shop a few doors down every morning. What if I bring one by here as well? That's worth a buck a box, right?"

"You drive a hard bargain, Ty," Mr. Harper said, extending a hand. "But you got yourself a deal!"

"And one more thing," Ty said, not wanting to part with any more upfront money if he could help it. "Is there any way to put that on store credit until I get paid at the end of this week?"

"Come up with unorthodox ways to solve the problem. When you look at the problem, think if there is a way to flip the problem upside down: can I flip the instinctive way I would handle this problem upside down in order to find a better result? Have a willingness to step away from obvious answers and what instinct is telling you, and ask: what is my imagination telling me?

"Bring imagination to the surface, say to yourself: 'How would Picasso solve this problem? Or how would Steve Jobs solve this problem? Or how would Oprah Winfrey solve this problem? Or how would President Obama solve this problem?'"

Josh Linkner,
CEO/Managing Partner, Detroit Venture Partners

THE FOURTH PRINCIPLE OF SUCCESS:
Overcoming Objections

On his third morning on the job, Ty realized he was going to need to accelerate his marketing plan if he was ever going to make any real money as a paperboy. This revelation came to him as he checked the mail after delivering to his nine customers, and saw his first paycheck from the *Sunnydale Sentinel.*

While it was true he made three dollars for each subscribing customer — $27 total — there were deductions for taxes, for the company delivering his stack of papers every morning, even for his messenger bag! In the end, the amount he had to deposit in the bank was just a little over $23, or $2.56 per customer. It was only twenty-four cents less per house, but the realization inspired him to think longer, and harder, about how to approach his new business venture.

With his messenger bag still slung over his shoulder, he got on his trusty bike and rode right back into town. His favorite bank teller, Carol, was happy to see him back again, particularly when she saw the *Sunnydale Sentinel* logo on his weekly paycheck.

"Look at you," she said, nodding toward the messenger bag on his shoulder. "Come to deposit your first paycheck?"

"Nope," Ty said, grinning. "I'm here to cash it."

Carol raised her eyebrows. "We're going in the wrong direction again, aren't we, Ty?"

"It may look like it," Ty said as Carol began handing him back $23.65 beneath her glass teller window, "but I look at it this way: I've got nine base houses I can use to generate income each week. If I save half that money every week, I'm still moving toward my goal. Meanwhile, I can use the rest of the money to make *more* money."

"Oh?" Carol asked, perking up. "That's great news! I've been trying to get you to shift your savings into one of our other great investment accounts. I'm glad you finally saw the light and decided to —"

"No," he grinned, waving her off. "I'm going to invest it in *me!*"

"How so, Ty?"

"Well, every week I'm going to use half my 'starter fund' to invest in my business. Repairs on my bike, rain gear, more red bags so nobody's paper gets wet, that kind of thing."

Carol nodded. "You think it will help?"

"It has to!" Ty insisted, folding his money and putting it in his pocket. He had a feeling it wouldn't last long enough to stay nice and flat in his wallet. "It's my senior year and this is the only job I can think of that won't interfere with my schoolwork. But it has to do what a job does, and that means make money. I can't do that with nine houses!"

Carol laughed. "No, you sure can't."

He turned to leave, but was suddenly inspired. He turned back to the window. "Can I have ten of this in quarters?" he asked, sliding a crisp bill back over to Carol.

"Sure," she said, exchanging it for a brand-new ten-dollar roll. "What for?"

"I just realized I don't have enough extra papers, so I'm going to buy a few dozen and use them to make the hard sell on some new customers."

"Great idea," she said as he pocketed the roll of quarters. "Good luck, Ty!"

He paused, about to correct her, and she winked.

"Sorry," she said, correcting herself. "Good luck investing in yourself!"

Ty hit the street, dropping his quarters in every *Sunnydale Sentinel* machine he saw. By the time he'd gone through his ten dollars he had twenty fresh copies to use in his latest sales pitch. But that was just the beginning.

"Hi, Chelsea!" he said as he walked into the drugstore.

"Hey, paperboy," she greeted him. She nodded at his bag. "How did those cards work out?"

"Great!" he said, joining her in the greeting-card aisle. "So great I want to get some more."

"Super," she said, tapping a fresh stack of multi-card boxes. "I was hoping you'd say that, because I ordered a few new styles."

"Yeah?" Ty said, impressed she'd remembered him.

She handed him a few cards. "I remembered you said you were a paperboy, and tossing them on front porches and welcome mats. This design has a row of houses I thought would be appropriate. This other box says 'Welcome' — you know, for folks moving into the neighborhood."

"Awesome!" Ty said. "I hadn't thought of that. People are always moving in and out these days."

With a nod, she continued: "And this third box just says 'Greetings,' which I thought could work with anything. So…how'd I do?"

"Great!" he said, following her up to the sales counter and grabbing a few new pens along the way. "Maybe I'll make you my business partner if I ever get more than nine houses on my route."

"I think we make a great team!" Chelsea said, making Ty blush. Risking a glance at her pretty face, Ty realized he wasn't the only one turning red.

"More passport photos?" she asked.

He nodded, but then looked down at his grubby T-shirt. "I'm kind of a mess, though…" he mumbled.

"No worries," she said, tapping some keys on her computer. "We keep them on file for a year so I'll just use your old photo to print the new ones. How many this time?"

He thought of his budget and added up what was left minus the boxes of greeting cards and new pens. "Let's do twenty for now," he said, figuring he'd need one for each of the extra papers he'd just bought. "And I'll grab some more each week."

"Wow!" Chelsea chuckled. "If this keeps up, you'll be running the *Sunnydale Sentinel* by Christmas."

"I don't want to run it," he replied, remembering the college semesters he was saving up for. "But stock options wouldn't hurt!"

Ty took the long way home, consulting the sheet of addresses to see where he might find some opportunities for sales. He started close to home, having realized if he focused on one street per week, or even per month — if it took that long — he could lock down more people than he could by running scattershot through his lists.

He rolled his bike to a stop in front of the first house on his list. He smiled. It was Mr. Johnson's house. Mr. Johnson was very fastidious man, and he loved a deal. No wonder he hadn't subscribed to the paper — yet!

His yard was spotless, with leaves raked and bagged along the curb. The American flag waved from a holder on his roof and on his porch were wicker chairs with soft cushions and matching throw pillows. But in the yard, his hose lay coiled, faded and leaky. The grass beneath the hose was a moldy yellow from overwatering.

Ty smiled, not at the old man's predicament, but at the solution he knew he'd find in the good old *Sunnydale Sentinel*. Sitting on the curb, he opened one of his papers and combed through each section, finally finding a flyer from Harper's Hardware Store.

Inside was a coupon for a new hose. It cost $9.99, and it was half as bulky as Mr. Johnson's current hose, and twice as long. Next to it was a coupon for a hose hanger for $4.99, if you bought the hose. This way, Mr. Johnson could loop his hose from a hanger on the side of his house instead of laying it on the grass and ruining the patch beneath.

Ty carefully tore out the coupon and used one of his new pens to circle both coupons and write in the margin: "A great buy for your yard!" Then he opened up a new greeting card — the kind with houses lined up on them, courtesy of Chelsea's great memory — and wrote inside: "Dear Mr. Johnson, I noticed your old hose had a leak, and found you an offer for a new one in today's paper. Imagine the deals you could find in the *Sunnydale Sentinel* every day — if only you were a subscriber! — Your Future Paperboy, Ty Chandler." He slid a picture of himself inside the card, then the card inside a new paper, then the paper inside a red bag, and tossed it onto the welcome mat.

Two houses down, he spotted a broken washing machine sitting on Mrs. Cooper's front porch. Knowing she was on a fixed income and wouldn't be able to afford a brand new one, he found a used one in good condition in the classified ads. He tore the page out of the paper and circled the ad with his pen before writing her a note and slipping it inside her free paper, which he tossed squarely onto her porch.

It happened to be recycling day and, pedaling past the end of Mr. and Mrs. Ketchum's driveway, he saw a green bin full of empty plastic bottles. He noticed they were all Power Punch, a popular sports drink.

Smiling to himself, he returned to his newspaper and, sure enough, found a "buy one six-pack, get the second free" coupon for Power Punch at the Sunnydale Grocery Store.

Tearing it out, he circled it and wrote a note. Inserting a picture into his greeting card, he folded up a paper, bagged it, tossed it, and moved on. And on and on. By late afternoon, he'd gotten rid of all twenty of his free papers and blanketed nearly the whole neighborhood. He gave a complimentary newspaper, a personalized note, and at least some type of opportunity provided by the *Sunnydale Sentinel*. Whether it was a toothpaste coupon or a classified ad or a free trip to the local miniature golf course, every paper contained some kind of treat for potential subscribers.

Now all he had to do was wait. Legs tired from the long day, he parked his bike back home, but he didn't want to miss any opportunities. He had a quick sandwich inside, grabbed the rake, and set about pretending to work in the yard, hoping one of his potential customers might spot the address he'd provided in every greeting card and wander by, just to see who this crazy young man who'd given them a free newspaper might be.

It happened just before sunset. Mr. Johnson approached, waving his folded paper energetically. "You there," he said, as Ty smiled and leaned on his rake. "What's the meaning of this?"

Mr. Johnson was a widower, in his seventies. He wore his usual "uniform" around the neighborhood: sweatpants and a yellow T-shirt under a brown golf sweater.

"Hi, Mr. Johnson," said Ty.

"Don't you 'Hi, Mr. Johnson' me, young man. Are you implying my hose is old and leaking?"

Ty laughed. "Well, it is!"

"That may be," Mr. Johnson admitted. "But maybe I like it that way."

"I know you, Mr. Johnson," Ty said, shaking his head. "That spotless lawn? You don't want a water stain on it, even if it *is* around the corner of the house."

"You been snoopin' around my house, boy?"

Ty held his hands up playfully, as if in surrender. "No, no, it's just… you can see it from the street, Mr. Johnson! I just thought a new hose would come in handy. I'm trying to help."

Mr. Johnson looked away, as if considering the offer, and then back again. "You know they took my driver's license away last year," he said, shaking his head. "My eyesight's not so great anymore. I haven't been able to get out and buy a new hose."

Ty felt bad. "I didn't know," he said. "I didn't mean—"

Mr. Johnson waved a hand. "You couldn't know," he said. "I just…I haven't been able to do a few of the things I should be doing for the house."

"I can pick up a new hose for you," Ty offered, suddenly inspired. Mr. Johnson narrowed his eyes. "What is this, some kind of joke?"

Ty shook his head, nodding toward the open garage. "I've got my bike," he said. "I can swing by the hardware store tomorrow morning, pick it up, and drop it off. No biggie."

"I couldn't ask you to do that," Mr. Johnson said.

"You didn't. I offered."

Mr. Johnson pursed his lips, and then nodded. "Well," he said, "since you're offering…" He reached inside his jacket pocket and pulled out a twenty-dollar bill, plus Ty's coupon from that morning.

"The hose is only ten dollars," Ty said.

"I know that," said Mr. Johnson, turning to leave. "The other ten is for my first week's subscription to the *Sunnydale Sentinel*. I assume that's enough to cover it?" he said, winking.

"Perfect!" said Ty. As he watched Mr. Johnson walk away, he realized he'd just sold his first subscription!

"You have to put your head down and lean forward. Life has its tough moments. You have to recognize they're out there. The measure of the person isn't how he or she deals with success—that's easy. It's how you deal with setbacks. Life is full of them.

"But if you believe that you are pursuing the right course of action, then you need to have fortitude and have the strength to drive on. You have to keep trying to learn, keep trying to improve, keep trying to do better, and achieve your objective."

General David Petraeus,
former director of the CIA

THE FIFTH PRINCIPLE OF SUCCESS:

Adding Value, Reducing Costs

"You feeling all right?"

Ty looked up from arranging the bills in his wallet and peered back at Chelsea, the helpful drugstore cashier. "Never better. Why?"

"Chicken soup?" she asked, tapping the tops of the two cans he'd slid forward on the sales counter.

Ty blushed. *Why did she have to notice everything?* Not that he was complaining. It was nice to have someone pay attention to him for a change, particularly somebody so pretty.

"One of my new customers, Mrs. Archer, had a couple of empty boxes of cough syrup in her recycling bin this morning so I figure she's not feeling so hot. She lives alone and probably shouldn't be driving, so I thought I'd swing some by now that school's over for the day."

Chelsea smiled. "That's sweet of you," she said, ringing up the soups. "It's gonna get expensive if you keep this up."

"They're buy one, get one free," he replied, a little defensively.

She laughed. "No, don't get me wrong, Ty, you're a very good shopper. But weren't you in here buying duct tape for somebody yesterday?"

He nodded. "I just wanted to seal up the leak in Mr. Randolph's downspout."

"And the day before that, wasn't it licorice for someone or another?"

"Mrs. Carlson's nephew is in town."

She wagged a finger as she took a five-dollar bill for the two cans of soup. "I know you want to be successful at your new job, Ty, but at what cost?"

"Whaddya mean?"

"I mean, a dollar for licorice here, two bucks for duct tape there, a few cans of soup — this is eating into your profits, my friend."

"That's where you're wrong," Ty insisted, pulling a series of bank envelopes from his messenger bag, each carefully labeled. "It's traditional in any business to spend up to a quarter of profits on operating expenses. I'm just divvying up mine differently than, say, some big corporation might."

He spread out the four envelopes on the sales counter so Chelsea could see their labels: Supplies, Surplus, Sales, and Service. Each envelope started with a ten-dollar bill, which Ty either replenished each week or "rolled over" from the last week.

"Supplies?" Chelsea asked, tapping the corresponding envelope with a manicured finger.

"My red delivery bags, the greeting cards you sell me, that kind of stuff," Ty explained. "'Surplus' is kind of a savings plus a slush fund, so if I'm running short on funds for supplies I can dip into that instead of going to the bank for more. Or if something pops up — if my bike gets a flat tire — I'll have money to cover it. The 'Sales' envelope is what I use to get more customers; it's for buying extra newspapers to deliver for free each week, that kind of thing."

"And 'Service'?" Chelsea asked.

He slid the two cans of soup into his messenger bag. "That's where you come in. If I can do something for all my customers every day, to make them happier, they'll tell a few people about it. Who will they tell? Usually a neighbor or friend, and when they say, 'Your paperboy did *what?*' hopefully they'll want to get in on that as well."

Chelsea stood back, eyes wide. "I stand corrected," she said. "So, rather than spending money, this is part of your operating capital."

"Right. I'm putting it back into the business each week."

"Is that sustainable?"

"How do you mean?"

"I mean, if you keep investing in your business, how much can it grow?"

Ty shrugged. "Until I reach my goal."

"And then what?" she challenged, as if enjoying herself. "You're gonna keep bringing chicken soup and licorice to *all* your customers?"

"Well," he said. "I mean, I'll taper down once I reach my goal."

She laughed. "We tried that," she said, pointing to a bowl of candy next to the cash register. It was full of round, pink-and-white-striped peppermints wrapped in plastic, the kind you'd get in a restaurant on the way out the door. He'd never really noticed it before; peppermints weren't his favorites.

"What do you mean?" he asked.

"We put this bowl of candy here when we first opened," she said, grabbing a peppermint and popping it in her mouth. Suddenly Ty's stomach growled and he reached for one as well. She laughed. "We figured, you know, put it out for a few weeks, no biggie, how much could it cost, right?"

"Right."

"Wrong," she laughed. "Folks got used to it. Everyone who stops in here grabs a piece, and not just customers. The mailman, the UPS guy, folks asking for directions, they all grab a piece, chomp it down, grab another for the road on their way out the door. Moms grab a handful for their purse, old ladies grab a handful for their sweater pockets, kids grab double handfuls — it's unreal!"

"It's not the same," he said.

"You don't think so?" she asked, as if she already knew the answer to her own question.

"It's just a little candy," he insisted.

She clicked her tongue and shook her head.

"Why are you shaking your head?" he asked. "How many pieces do you go through a day?"

"Pieces?" Chelsea blurted, reaching under the counter to pull out a giant bag of peppermint candies. It was nearly as big as Ty's messenger bag, the kind you might buy in a bulk food stores. "Try *bags*. We go through two of these bags per day!"

"Get out of here," Ty said.

"Each of these bags is twelve dollars," she said. "So you're looking at twenty-five bucks a day, basically just gone. Evaporated into thin air."

"But people love it."

"So?" she asked. "You think they come in here just for the free candy?"

Ty considered her question. "I think it's part of the reason why they come in," he said.

She rolled her eyes. "How do you figure?"

"Well," he said, trying to figure it all out for himself at the same time. "Why do any of us buy anything? I mean, there are three drugstores in town, so why do I keep coming back here?"

"It must be the awesomely cute cashier," Chelsea teased.

"That's one reason," he confessed, feeling his cheeks grow warm. "But there are some other reasons." He began ticking them off on his fingers. "It's close to my house, the prices are reasonable, you have what I need, I can get my questions answered, it's small so I don't have to go all over the place to find what I'm looking for, it's quiet, never very crowded, I can get in and out of here pretty quickly —"

She laughed, interrupting him. "At least, when the cashier doesn't bust your chops about your business model, right?"

"But see," he said, "that's another reason to shop here. A lot of cashiers would sell me greeting cards and licorice and chicken soup and never care what I was doing with them. They'd just ring it up, hand me the bag, and go back to chomping their gum. Lots of folks are like that."

"But enough to keep coming in?" she pressed him.

"You guys do all right," he said. Then again, he and Chelsea had been talking for nearly ten minutes and nobody else had come into the store.

"I guess," she admitted. "But my point is, we tried to stop giving away free candy by the cash register a few months ago — you know, to keep our costs down. And people went crazy. They were really, really mad. In the end, we had to bring the candy dish back out!"

He sighed. "So you're saying I'm going to have to keep up whatever I'm doing to both get business and to *keep* business?"

She shrugged. "I guess that's the cost of doing business," she said. "I guess what I'm saying is, just pace yourself."

"You're right," he admitted. "I guess I didn't think it all the way through."

"Neither did we," she said, refilling the candy jar.

"You could always try taking the candy jar away for good," he suggested.

"And face the wrath of a dozen customers per hour?" she said. "No thanks."

"Some things you just have to do," he said.

"Like what?"

"Like have air conditioning and restrooms for your customers."

"Well, sure," she said. "You can't not do those things."

"Lots of places make you use a key for the restroom," he said. "Like the drugstore closer to school. I don't go there anymore, because it's always a hassle."

"I know why they do it," she said.

"Me too," he said. "So kids won't steal stuff in there. But I don't steal their stuff, and it makes me feel like they don't trust me, so why should I give them my money — ever?"

"You've got a point," she agreed.

"And that other drugstore, over on Elm Street?" he added. "It smells like mothballs, so I don't go there."

"What about Dilbert's Drugs on Chase Street?" she pressed. "That's not far from your school."

"No," he admitted. "But they're always running out of something, or following you around the store if you hang out too long. I guess there are more reasons not to shop at those other drugstores and more plusses why I should shop here."

"I wish we could fit that on our sign out front," she said. "It could be our new motto!"

Ty hoisted his messenger bag, heavier now with the cans of chicken soup inside. "Well," he said, nodding toward the late-afternoon light outside the drugstore window, "I'd better get these to Mrs. Archer if she's going to have one for dinner tonight."

"That's really sweet of you, Ty," said Chelsea.

"It's just business," he insisted.

She shook her head. "I know *you* think so, but it's more than that to your customers. And it's the kind of thing that, even when you're no longer a paperboy, will be good for any business you get into."

"Like working for a drugstore?" he teased.

"Don't fool yourself, Ty," she said. "I don't see you working *for* anyone much longer. One day, we'll all be working for you."

Ty hopped on his bike and headed for home. As he pedaled, Chelsea's words rattled around in his brain.

He knew it wasn't wrong to have an operating budget for his rotating expenses. There were things he needed every week, or at least every month, to reach his goal of signing up everyone in his territory — extra-strong bags, greeting cards, passport photos — and making customer service a top priority couldn't be wrong.

But Chelsea had a point about growth and scaling. Could he afford to drop off chicken soup and duct tape and licorice when he had more than a dozen subscribers? When he had two dozen? Three? Four? And Chelsea was right about another thing, too: he couldn't stop providing excellent customer service once he reached his goal.

That would be a bait-and-switch tactic, and not only was it a bad way to do business; it was also not the way he *wanted* to do business.

As he walked up to Mrs. Archer's front door, a can of soup in each hand, he wondered if there was any way he could still provide service — and add value — without eating too far into his profits.

"Why, Tyler!" said Mrs. Archer as she answered his knock at the door. Her nose was red and stuffy, and she held a crumpled tissue in one hand. "What's the meaning of this?"

"I saw the cough-syrup boxes in your recycling bin," he explained. "I thought you might not be able to get out, so I brought you some soup."

"Oh, my!" she said. "How sweet of you. Thanks to you, I know what I'm having for dinner."

"Is there anything else you need?"

She shook her head, and then paused. "Actually," she said, nodding toward the clouds overhead, "the weatherman says it's supposed to rain, and my gutters are loaded with leaves. I meant to clean them out sooner, but then I came down with the flu. Can you…?"

He smiled. "Clean your gutters before the storm? Of course, Mrs. Archer."

"Mr. Archer's not very handy," she said, whispering as if he might hear. "And he's away on business all week, so…"

"Happy to," Ty said, slipping off his messenger bag as Mrs. Archer led him to the garage.

"Everything you need's in there," she said as she held the cans of chicken soup. "I'd gladly whip you up some soup once you're done."

"Those are for you," he insisted, grabbing a ladder and a pair of gloves. "My mom will have dinner waiting for me when I'm done."

Mrs. Archer coughed, tugging her robe tighter. "Be careful," she warned from the doorway.

He smiled and propped the ladder against the gutter above the garage. As he climbed up, pausing halfway to tug on the gloves, Ty realized he'd just found a way to still provide excellent service to his customers, without costing him anything at all. Well, anything but time.

And, as he realized when he looked at the stuffed gutters, apparently lots of it!

"I think the most important issue at hand is whether the professional has the interest of the client first and foremost in their mind when they start the discussion, or if it is a self-serving conversation. Inevitably, cross-selling will be a priority for a lot of firms. But what makes a difference in the eyes of the client is whether the client believes the professional is raising the possibility of a broader relationship or selling a wider set of services. If the client believes the professional is offering this truly as a way to solve sophisticated, complex issues that the client cares about, it will be perceived differently than if client believes the professional is raising these issues as a way to increase his or her own profit or credit.

What clients tell me is that when they find an advisor who truly has a deep understanding of their business and their situation, that's when they are willing to entertain buying additional services."

Heidi Gardner,
lecturer, Harvard Law School

THE SIXTH PRINCIPLE OF SUCCESS:
Creating Raving Fans

"Happy Halloween!"

Ty sat at the breakfast table after his morning route — fifty-seven customers on three streets in the subdivision, and counting. He was filling out a stack of cheap Halloween cards from Discount Drug Mart.

He'd picked up three new boxes on the way home from school the day before, with twenty cards in each. They featured various seasonal designs like smiling jack-o'-lanterns, flying witches, bony skeletons, and kids trick-or-treating. Because of Ty's and his mom's busy schedules, they were the only sign of the upcoming holiday in the entire house.

Ty's mom opened the refrigerator door and grabbed the orange juice. "Aren't you a little early, Ty?" she grumbled. "It's only October twenty-ninth."

Eileen Chandler was a realtor with Streets of Sunnydale, a realty office downtown. She liked to say: "The early realtor beats the lazy one into the office every Monday and to the bank every Friday." It was a credo she lived by, waking up early every morning and heading into the office long before Ty left for school.

She was popular with her clients and extremely successful, landing on her feet — and then some — after a nasty divorce from Ty's father when Ty was just in middle school which had left her deep in debt. She paid off all her credit card bills and the house was nearly paid for as well. As soon as it was, she promised, she'd rent it out and they'd move somewhere nicer.

Ty smiled, sealing another card and adding it to his growing "done" stack. "I know, but I'm inviting my customers to a 'Tricks and Sweets' party

47

in Hampton Squares Park this Friday and I want to get in the mood, so…
Happy Halloween!"

She laughed, pouring a cup of fresh coffee from the pot he'd brewed
for her after he finished his route. "Well, Happy Halloween to you, too."
She looked around the kitchen, which, as every year, was devoid of orange
and black garlands or cardboard witches or even a flickering jack-o'-lantern.
"I guess I've been too busy to decorate this year."

"It's okay," he said, waving a greeting card festooned with dancing
skeletons. "I'm funneling all my holiday spirit into my party."

Ty's mom sat down across from him and frowned. "You're going
trick-or-treating with some customers?" she asked, confused.

Ty smiled. "Not quite," he said, handing her the card he'd just finished,
which bore the following message inside:

Happy Halloween! And greetings from Ty, your favorite paperboy!

*Please join me for my first annual "Tricks and Sweets" extravaganza at
the Hampton Squares Park this Friday night, Halloween, from 5 to 7. Enjoy
complimentary candy, spooky music, and family-friendly fun before, or after,
your trick-or-treating festivities. See you there! —Ty*

"The paper's putting this on?" she asked, handing the card back so Ty
could seal it in an orange envelope and add it to his "done" pile.

"No, I am."

Ty's mom looked up from her coffee. "Why?"

Ty shrugged. "Well, I've increased my customer base by, like, six
hundred percent, and I want to thank them for subscribing. Halloween
seemed like as good a time as any."

"How come?"

"How come Halloween?"

His mom smiled. "No, how come you're throwing a party in the first
place?"

"Customer appreciation," he explained. "I want them to know I
appreciate them and I want to get to know them a little better. Plus the
park is perfect since it is right in the middle of my customer base and no
one has to drive or park or anything."

"I dunno, Ty," his mother said, setting down her coffee mug. "Sounds expensive."

"Not really," he explained. "I found a Gamma Man costume at the thrift shop for ten bucks. The rental fee for using the gazebo in Hampton Squares Park for two hours is only forty-five dollars, and I ordered bulk candy online for fifty-five dollars and two hundred treat sacks for twenty dollars. I figure this way I can show my appreciation, have some fun, get everybody together, hand out some candy, and not make such a big dent in my operating budget."

Ty's mom nodded and sat back. "Wow, I had no idea your subscriber base had grown so big," she said, beaming with pride. "That's really great, Ty."

He shrugged. "Well, it's been a lot of work but it's finally starting to pay off."

"I know it's your senior year and you're saving for college, son, but are you sure you have time for all of this with school and everything else you've got going on?"

Ty reassured her. "I'm actually putting in a lot fewer hours than my friends who have after-school and weekend jobs at Burger Barn and the grocery store, and a lot fewer hours than I would have if I'd stayed at the movie theater. And now that my subscriber base is growing, I'm making more than those guys."

She beamed, tapping the stack of sealed envelopes he'd been working on all morning. "Not if you keep spending money on these," she said, "and on bulk candy from the Internet, and renting out park gazebos on Friday nights."

Ty shrugged. Even with the added expense, he was still ahead of his projections for the month and well within his ultimate goal. "It's just the cost of doing business, Mom."

"Perhaps, Ty, but your friends who work at Burger Barn don't spend money to do their jobs, do they?"

"Sure they do," he insisted. "They have to buy their own work uniforms, which get deducted from their paychecks. Then they have to buy new sneakers every few weeks when the old ones wear out from standing on their feet all day, and super-heavy-duty laundry detergent to get the smell of French fries and burger grease out of their uniforms. They have to have cars to get them to and from work, and put gas in their cars, and —"

Ty's mom laughed. "Okay, okay," she said, holding her hands up in surrender. "I get your point, but I just don't want you spending all your profits to gain more subscribers, only to turn around and spend all your profits to thank them. That's no way to run a business, Ty, *or* save money for college."

"Well, I'm still a long way off from my goal," he explained. "And it's not *all* my profits. And besides, aren't you the one who's always saying that you have to spend money to make money? I mean, isn't that why you bought that new tablet, to keep up with clients and sales and new deals? Isn't that why you buy nice suits and go to the dry cleaner a couple of times a week? That's not cheap either, Mom."

She laughed, looking at him as if seeing him for the first time all morning. "I guess I just never thought of it that way," she said. "I suppose every job has requirements that aren't necessarily listed in the job description."

"Sure," Ty agreed. "I don't have to do all this stuff, but I've got a goal and I want to reach it. And it's like your new tablet or business suits. You can't really tell if someone's choosing you as their realtor because you have the latest technology and always look professional, but I think we both know it makes you different from the competition."

She nodded. "But you don't have any competition, Ty. You're the only paperboy with this territory."

"True, Mom, but think about it this way: Your new tablet is my competition."

She tilted her head. "How?"

"More and more folks are reading the paper online," he explained. "They can get it on their cell phone, their tablets, their laptops, and desktops. It's quicker, easier, and simpler that way. So I've got to convince my customers that reading the actual paper, live and in person, is better than reading it online."

"But is it?"

"Not for everybody," he admitted. "The guy I took over the route from was right when he said 'Nobody reads the newspaper anymore.' What he meant was the actual paper at the breakfast table. And he's right. If you're busy and just want the headlines, sure, reading the paper on your tablet makes more sense. But there's a lot of content that's not available online, or that is compromised by the online experience."

"Like what?"

"Well, you can't get the same coupons online, and lots of our neighbors are interested in that kind of thing. I tell them all the time — it's part of my pitch — that if you get the paper for the coupons alone you'd save twice as much every week as the paper costs. Half of them are older and retired, and they even have a problem with the ones you can print: the ink for their printer often costs more than the savings they're getting. They like to study the classifieds and it's easier in print; plus, they grew up reading the paper like you and Dad did, and that's the most comfortable way for them."

"Great argument, Ty. But how do you let them know all that?"

He laughed. "That's what I've been trying to do with the red bags and free papers, Mom, and the passport photos and greeting cards. The paper doesn't really advertise, at least not in my territory, so I've got to spend money to make money."

Ty's mother nodded, but seemed unconvinced. "So, tell me this, Ty — wouldn't it be smarter to invite folks who *aren't* customers to your Halloween party? I mean, why waste money on folks who are already subscribing?"

"I thought about that, Mom, but I have three or four times as many nonsubscribers as I do subscribers. And everyone's a neighbor here, so I'm hoping that when folks head out to my party, their neighbors will wonder where they're going. And when they ask, my customers will tell them: 'The paperboy's throwing us a party!' And maybe they'll wonder why they're not getting their papers delivered as well!"

Ty's mom finished her coffee and stood, ready to meet her own day. Ty wouldn't be far behind her. Even after delivering nearly sixty papers and stuffing as many envelopes, he still had pop quizzes and term papers and oral reports to think about, not to mention a full day of school.

"I just don't want you to get overwhelmed, Ty," she said, squeezing his shoulder as she passed him on her way out of the kitchen. "I wish there was some way I could help."

"Well," he replied, turning in his chair to face her, "I could use some help passing out 'Trick or Sweets' bags Friday night."

Her face fell as she paused in the kitchen doorway. "I wish I could, Ty, but I've got that open house at the Johnson's place that night and, well…"

"It's okay, Mom," Ty said, reassuring her. "I was only kidding."

* * * *

"Happy Halloween!" In his red and yellow Gamma Man costume, Ty mingled, greeting subscribers and handing out black-and-orange treat sacks full of chocolates, gummy bears, licorice, and candy corn. Most of his subscribers had decided to show up — if for no other reason, it seemed, than to have an excuse to go out as an adult on Halloween.

"I haven't been out trick-or-treating in years," said Mrs. Johnson, looking dapper in fuzzy blue slippers and a pink housecoat. She had rollers in her hair.

"Who are you supposed to be?" asked Ty, handing her a treat sack.

"Why," she said, waving her walker as she danced a quick two-step for him, "an old lady, of course!"

Ty laughed and handed out some more treat sacks, trying to recognize faces behind masks and other disguises. Then again, he didn't know all of his subscribers, only the ones he'd done little favors for along the way, or dropped off "treats" for long before Halloween.

The mood was festive: the streets of Hampton Squares were alive with flickering pumpkins on every porch and blinking orange and purple string lights in the windows.

Ty had arrived early and wound blinking orange lights around the gazebo while adorning its four steps with flickering jack-o'-lanterns he'd carved himself. Inside the gazebo a band called Cartwheels played scary Halloween songs, everything from "Flying Purple People Eater" to "Monster Mash." They were really just four guys from Ty's school who played at local senior centers and talent shows on the weekend, but they were perfect for the night's festivities — and cheap, too!

As the sun set and darkness fell, more people arrived and Ty hustled from group to group, handing out bags and shaking hands and thanking one and all for subscribing to the paper.

For Ty, it was more than just a chance to thank his subscribers for being customers. He hadn't really had an excuse to get dressed up and go trick-or-treating for years. It felt good to wear a costume again, and dance to "Ghostbusters" with the little kids in front of the gazebo.

As the night wore on and more and more people showed up, Ty ran short of candy. He'd hidden the big box of bulk candy in the gazebo behind the band but it was getting low and he'd run out of treat sacks long ago.

After pouring the last of the candy into his messenger bag, minus the treat sacks, Ty was basically handing out pieces of candy to anyone who asked — but it wouldn't last long, and he still had forty minutes left in his party!

He was on his last few pieces of candy, looking at a bunch of eager kids' hands and no way to fill them, when a sprightly witch cackled beside him, sliding a giant pillowcase off her back and plopping it on the ground.

"Here we go, kiddies," she said in her best witch voice, dishing out fun-size candy bars, bubblegum, and lollipops with one hand while waving a plastic broom with the other. "Trick or sweets!"

The kids giggled and munched, dancing as the band played another spooky tune.

"Thanks," Ty said, wiping his forehead with his bright-red Gamma Man glove. "You just saved my radioactive butt back there!"

"Don't worry about it, Ty," said a familiar voice. The witch slid her big floppy hat back.

"Mom?" he gasped.

"Shhhh," she said, raising a black-gloved finger to her lips. "Don't spoil it for the kiddies."

"How'd you know I'd need more candy?" he asked as she siphoned half the contents of the orange pillowcase into his messenger bag.

"It's Halloween, Ty," she said, giving him an affectionate hug. "Everyone always runs out of candy. Besides, it was half price at Discount Drug Mart, so I saved you a bundle."

"You're *charging* me for it?"

"Hey, family is family," she teased, pushing her hat back down as another wave of kids approached, hands out. "And business is business. Besides, don't worry; you can pay me back in installments!"

Ty couldn't argue with that. And after all, he would have paid double for fresh candy reinforcements in order to keep his customers and their hungry kids happy!

"I often counsel people to really understand if and how their business model creates customer need. You need to know if you're going to be able to fulfill good economics per products sold, and if the overall business model is successful. A lot of the business plans that don't work get created around settings where people are dissatisfied with status quo. They really don't like having to pay fifteen percent to a distributor in order to get the product from the manufacturer to the retail outlet. But they don't understand that just being unhappy with the status quo doesn't mean you can rip the distributor out of the model and make it work. You have to make sure the model that you create has viability, so that every time you sell a product, you know how much money you are bringing in, and what the cost and scale is. It's more about 'How do I make money out of this?' rather than 'I wish the world in this area were different.'"

William Kerr,
professor at Harvard Business School

THE SEVENTH PRINCIPLE OF SUCCESS:

Crushing It with Consistency

The alarm bleated and Ty groaned, rolling over in bed to turn it off. He knew he should get up, but it was mid-November now, the air dark and chilly, and his warm sheets felt so good tangled around his body. Besides, there was always the snooze button, and if that went ignored, he'd set his cell phone alarm as a third backup for ten minutes later. Not to mention he was half an hour early to start his route anyway!

Ty didn't believe in leaving anything to chance. Before the next snooze button alarm rang, he sighed, rose, and turned it off, as well as his cell phone alarm. His room was neat and orderly, everything in its place and a place for everything.

Not that things didn't go haywire from time to time; they did. This morning, in particular, would try Ty's patience more than any to date, but he wasn't aware of that as he stood up and rubbed the sleep from his eyes.

Like every morning, by five o'clock Ty was showered and downing a granola bar and can of iced coffee over the kitchen sink. But that was the last normal moment of his day! As he stepped outside and sauntered down to the curb, where his papers were dropped in a haphazard bundle, he frowned.

He had nearly one hundred houses on his route now, all up and down his territory, and he could tell at a glance that his stack was short a few papers.

This happened from time to time. Not often, but on those few times, protocol decreed that he call his dispatcher to alert the paper to the problem, and then wait for more papers. That often took up to two hours, and by that time he would already be in homeroom awaiting roll call.

Better to solve the problem himself. So he counted them, and sure enough, he was six papers short. He opened the garage and went straight for the bottom drawer of his mom's sewing table. She had cleaned it out for him when he got the job and now he used it for storing little odds and ends he often had the need for in a typical morning — rubber bands, paperclips, that kind of thing.

He always kept a few rolls of quarters there from his operating budget and grabbed one to feed into the nearest *Sunnydale Sentinel* box at the corner of Fifth and Main. Then he hopped on his bike, getting as far as the end of the drive before he realized he had a flat tire!

Ty promptly wheeled the bike back into the garage and grabbed his spare. He'd bought it secondhand for just such occasions. It wasn't as slick as his regular bike, but it was more than enough to get the job done until he got his "big bike" fixed, and it meant he would never miss out on a morning delivery.

Ty hadn't used it in a while, so he spent a few minutes making sure the tires had just the right amount of air, readjusting the seat, and hitting the spokes and chain with a little WD-40. Once it was road-ready, he was out the door and racing up to Main Street, cutting over to Fifth Street where there was a blue-and-white *Sunnydale Sentinel* box.

He cracked open his roll of quarters and fed two at a time into the machine, dragging one out each time before shutting the door and buying another copy, then five more, until he had all of his missing papers…plus one extra, just in case.

It wasn't proper procedure, but it was far more efficient than waiting for the paper to drop off the extras a full hour after he'd usually delivered them. Sure, it cost him three dollars of his own money, but it was well worth the inconvenience and expense to keep his clients happy.

He had a strict timeline to keep, and it posed a challenge with each new subscriber. A single wrinkle in his morning, from waking up late to a flat tire to missing papers, sent a ripple effect through his entire schedule.

Half his customers would never know if the paper got there a few minutes late. Many of them wouldn't even get up until long after Ty was sitting in first or second period, but many others would — and he couldn't afford to let a single customer down.

Not after working so hard to sign up each and every one!

He slid the papers into his messenger bag and raced back home, quickly folding and sliding each one into one of his trademark weatherproof, durable, recognizable red plastic bags. He knew he'd been running low all week, but he'd had a term paper due, and just hadn't gotten around to restocking his supply.

Now, as he neared the end of his stack, with five papers to go he ran out of red bags entirely. Sure, he could use the bags the paper provided each morning — he had plenty of those — but that wasn't his style.

As he bit his lower lip, he noticed the kitchen light was on inside the house. He walked back inside to find his mom hovering over the sink with her first cup of coffee.

"Morning, kiddo," she said. She was already dressed and ready for her day. When it came to raging workaholics, the apple didn't fall far from the tree. "What's up?"

"Oh, I just ran out of red bags and need to find replacements."

She clicked her tongue. "Isn't the paper supposed to provide you with bags?"

"They do, but they're so flimsy. I only need about five bags. Any ideas?"

She sighed. "Well, I just got some extra-large freezer bags you could use. They'd probably fit a paper, but they've got snowflakes on them."

Ty followed his mother to the pantry. "Those sound great."

"Well, I was going to use them for soups and chili this weekend, but…"

"I'll replace them by then," Ty told her, taking the box from her hand and kissing her on the cheek. "Promise!"

"Why don't you get the paper to reimburse you for all these extra expenses?" she asked as he paused in the doorway between the kitchen and the garage.

"Sure thing, Mom," he teased. "The same day you ask your realtor to reimburse you for all your tailored suits and fancy pens!"

His mom's laughter still ringing in his ears, Ty hustled back to the curb to wrap the last of his papers — albeit in snowflake-covered freezer baggies — and shove them into his messenger bag.

He checked his watch and frowned: five minutes behind schedule! On his regular bike he could have made up the lost minutes in no time, but on his backup bike it would be a struggle.

He sped off, knowing his route by heart, pedaling up and down each street in the dark, grateful for the streetlights and porch lights and the crescent moon lighting his way. If he'd been like other paperboys, he could have just streaked by, tossing papers willy-nilly onto lawns and porches, hitting screen door, shrubs, and porch swings as often as actually landing them near the doors.

But Ty set high standards for himself, even when they caused his heart to race and blood pressure to skyrocket in order to satisfy them.

Leaping on and off his bike at every house to carefully place the paper on the welcome mat might not have mattered to every customer, but enough of them had mentioned how nice it was that he couldn't stop now!

And so he hustled and leapt and strained and placed, and straightened and placed and strained and hustled some more to ensure that every house got what they had come to expect: a perfectly folded dry newspaper delivered, quite literally, to their front door.

Up one side of the street and down the other Ty went, until neither the crisp November chill nor his backup bike's rusty chain and wobbly pedals bothered him.

Halfway through his route he finally got back on schedule, smiling as he spotted his old friend, and sometime nemesis, waiting impatiently for her morning delivery.

"Thought you might be late," said Mrs. Carlton, sounding almost disappointed. She was a new customer all the way out on Sullivan Street, the last in his territory.

"Never!" he replied, riding his bike right up to her porch where she stood in matching pink slippers on her bottom step, clutching her bathrobe to her neck, as she did every day.

She accepted the paper with a smile. "I don't know how you do it, Ty," she said, wagging the paper playfully as he turned his bike around to head back and finish his route. "But I could set my watch by you every morning!"

"That's the idea," he said, waving over his shoulder. "Satisfaction guaranteed, or your paper's free the next morning."

"You had to give any away yet?" she teased.

He paused at the end of her drive. "Not yet," he boasted. "And I don't intend to, either."

"Don't fall prey to 'sunk costs' or an 'escalation of commitment' type of mentality. If you love the 'get your hands dirty' part of entrepreneurship and your venture is not working, but you already have another idea you'd like to pursue, just start your next startup. Or do something else that you've been meaning to do. Whatever you do, it's not going to be fun all the time, but my sense is that you always have a feeling when it's time to just call it quits. There's no shame in that."

Laura Huang,
assistant professor of management
and entrepreneurship, Wharton School

THE EIGHTH PRINCIPLE OF SUCCESS:
Scaling for Growth

One morning in mid-December, Ty was on Baker Street, not far from his house, his arms and legs tired from another long week of delivering the *Sunnydale Sentinel*, when he noticed a shadowy figure sitting on the front stoop.

Ty fixed a smile on his face and slowed to a stop in front of the house where the figure sat. He leaned his bike against a tree and approached cautiously, paper extended.

"Everything okay, Ms. March?" he asked.

"Just fine, Ty," said the middle-aged woman, looking prim and proper even at that early hour. "I was just wondering if you had a minute."

"Sure," he said, even though he still had to get back home, hop in the shower, and get ready for school. "What's up?"

Ms. March was one of his newer customers and he'd only been delivering to her for a few days. She was in her mid-fifties, a busy professional like his mom, her house big and spacious but looking a little rough around the edges.

"Now, I'm not sure if you can help me," she said, peering at him from behind big glasses with red frames that matched her auburn curls, "but this lawn is in pretty bad shape."

He followed her to the edge of the drive where, sure enough, the grass was an unruly inch or two too long.

"I can see that," he said good-naturedly. "I'm just wondering why you're telling your paperboy about your lawn."

"Come on now," she teased, nudging him with her shoulder. "You're much more than that. I heard from Ms. Simpson you cleaned out her gutters last week, and Mr. Farthington said you helped him clean out his shed the other weekend."

Ty's smile remained fixed, even as he tried to work up a fitting response. He could see where this was headed, and wondered what to do about it. He'd worked so hard at getting customers, giving away free papers and delivering little treats, doing odd jobs and making himself available for "extra duty" that, now that he'd nearly reached his goal and had over one hundred and fifty subscribers on his route, he wondered how he could keep it up with a full school schedule.

"Sure," he said. "I guess I could help…"

Then Ms. March dropped a bombshell that had never occurred to Ty, and would change his entire business model for the rest of his senior year, and for many years to come.

"Well, Ty, I'd pay you, of course," she said, so casually and sincerely that he knew immediately it wasn't a negotiating tactic. She meant it, and suddenly he understood the power of his position: by working only a few hours each morning, he had the opportunity to reach hundreds of potential customers he might be able to serve *after* school every day.

"It'd have to wait until the afternoon," he told her, heart pounding with the nearly endless possibilities that her offer had unleashed. "Would that be okay?"

"Sure," she said, scraping a fuzzy blue slipper across the top of the scruffy tall grass. "It's waited this long, so a few more hours wouldn't hurt!"

Ty thought about the encounter all day, mind whirring as he found it hard to concentrate on his regular classes. Somehow he made it to lunch where, rather than sitting in the cafeteria with his friends as he usually did he drifted into the computer lab.

"Hey, Ty!" beamed Mr. French, the computer teacher. "Come for a little extra credit?"

"Something like that," Ty said, finding an empty workstation and booting up the desktop. "I was wondering how many student credits it would cost me if I were to print up something."

"What, like a college application or something?" Mr. French asked. "A lot of seniors have been doing that this week."

"More like a flyer," Ty confessed.

Mr. French screwed up his face. "We talking color here?" he asked. "Or black and white?"

Ty laughed. "Black and white," he said, "but on color paper."

The computer teacher seemed relieved. "In that case," he said, taking Ty's student services card, "knock yourself out."

So Ty did. Using his favorite graphics design program and the brainstorming he'd been doing all day, Ty worked all lunch period to craft a simple, clear, concise flyer that would be cheap to reproduce each week, and garner him enough part-time jobs after school to double, even triple, his weekly paycheck.

It said simply:

Ty's Trees and Things!

For all your landscaping, hardware, and home care needs. From lawn mowing to tree trimming to running errands, let your local neighborhood handyman help you help yourself! Contact Ty at 555-393-3417 anytime, day or night, for all your "trees and things" needs.

After fiddling with a font here, placing an underline there, and correcting a few spelling mistakes, he printed fifty copies on bright lemon-yellow paper.

"'Ty's Trees and Things,' huh?" Mr. French mused, picking up a flyer from the quickly growing stack.

Ty nodded. "I've been delivering papers in the mornings before school and on weekends —" he began.

"They still do that?" Mr. French gasped, interrupting. "Deliver papers, I mean?"

"I get a lot of that," Ty told him, grinning. "Anyway, this morning a lady asked me to come back after school and mow her lawn, and I realized that's probably a pretty common need in my territory, so…"

"So you're scaling for growth, huh?"

Ty grabbed the last of his stack and stood with them pressed to his chest, the heat from the printer still warm on his Harding High T-shirt. "'Scaling for growth?' What do you mean?"

"It's a business principle where you adapt to new business opportunities and fold them into your old business model," his teacher explained. "So, you started delivering papers and took that as far as you could. Now you're assessing your schedule, time available, and consumer needs to adapt to change."

"Wow," Ty grinned as Mr. French handed him his student ID badge back, the credits for his printing session already deducted from his monthly account. "I'm doing all that?"

"You sure are," said Mr. French, waving the flyer in his hand for emphasis.

Ty reached for it, and Mr. French playfully yanked it out of reach. "Hey now," he said, "just because I don't live on your street doesn't mean I won't need your services. As a matter of fact, you should give me another one and I'll put it up in the teachers' lounge for you. You might get a lot of extra work that way."

Ty did just that, sliding the rest of his flyers into his backpack and keeping them safe all day until at last he was free, blitzing out the side door the minute the final bell had rung, leaping on his bike, and racing for home.

After a quick snack and a power drink, Ty changed into camouflage cargo pants, an old paint-stained T-shirt he wouldn't mind getting dirty, and ratty sneakers. Stacking his flyers on top of his red delivery bags for the next morning, he hopped on his backup bike and peddled back to Ms. March's house.

Not surprisingly, she was waiting outside, leaning on the porch railing with a cup of coffee in hand. "There he is!" she said, smiling as he leaned his bike against the railing and nodded. "How was school today?"

He smiled. "Things are kind of slow leading into Christmas break," he said, "so it's a good time for me to be helping folks out after school."

"Good," she said, stepping from the porch to lead him to the garage. "Because I might have let Ms. Philpots over on Sullivan Street know you were stopping by, and she wanted me to see if you had time to trim her rosebushes tomorrow!"

Ty laughed and reached for the lawnmower. "Only if you don't wear me out first, Ms. March," he replied. It took him five tries to get the lawnmower's engine running, and another thirty minutes to get the underside properly cleaned and the blade sharpened. He was tuckered out afterward, and that was before he'd started mowing the lawn!

Still, once he got started he was glad to be zipping along, creating a clean, tight pattern in full view of the street. More than one car slowed down, with the drivers rolling down their windows to ask how much he charged. Ty could have kicked himself for not bringing a few flyers along with him to hand out.

Even so, by the time he was through mowing Ms. March's lawn — and trimming her hedges and raking her leaves — he had several more projects lined up for that week, not including the tip from Ms. March about Mrs. Philpots!

As dusk began to fall and his day was finally at an end, Ty wheeled the lawnmower back into the garage. He had tidied up a little, making room for the lawnmower and arranging the products he'd use for its upkeep — oil, gas, WD-40, rags, and other paraphernalia — in neat piles. He stood, turning to find Ms. March beaming back at him.

"Ty, you're amazing!" she said, peering closer at the organized corner of her garage. "I've been meaning to clean this garage up for years, but just haven't gotten around to it. Maybe next week you can come back and organize it from head to toe?"

"I'd love to," he said, following her outside to survey her lawn. "Just let me know a good day for you."

"Any day is fine," she said, her voice trailing off as she followed the clean, smooth lines of the grass, closely trimmed, along the length of the drive. When they arrived at the sidewalk, she peered at the six garbage bags, full of raked leaves, waiting for the next day's trash pickup.

"And the lawn looks as good as the garage." She handed him three crisp twenty-dollar bills.

"What's this?" he asked, realizing he'd never quoted a price.

"Is that enough?" she asked, hand hovering over her pocketbook. "Most guys I hire charge twenty dollars an hour, right?"

"Right!" he said, quickly pocketing the money and realizing she'd paid him for three hours' work. "And I appreciate it, more than you know."

"Me too," she said, patting one of the garbage bags. "Really, Ty, you've gone over and above."

"Happy to, Ms. March," he said, hopping on his bike, mind reeling with the possibilities of his new business venture. "And let me know about next week!"

Pedaling home, Ty could hardly wait for the next morning, when he'd put the first of his new flyers in every other newspaper before delivering them.

By staggering the flyers out each week, he could be sure to hit all of his customers, but not every day, or even every other day. Once a week, he figured, would be plenty to remind his customers that when they needed something done, Ty would be ready for — and up to — the challenge!

"When I was getting ready to launch, I was told that when people land on your website, you're going to need media, you're going to need pictures and video. At the time I was watching the Carson Daly show before I'd go to bed, so I thought, "Maybe I should reach out to these NBC producers, and see if there's any chance that when Wings for Warriors launches, maybe we could be part of this show. So I literally cold called NBC and talked to people with Last Call with Carson Daly, and got on the show because Matthew McConaughey cancelled. It was the best timing in the world — just sheer luck. He had a nonprofit organization, so they were doing nonprofit week, so it just worked out. The night the segment aired we got $13,000 in online donations. It ran two other times, generating got $3,000 to $4,000 each time. But that night was an a-ha! moment. I realized I had created something that was going to be successful. That was four and a half years ago."

Anthony Ameen,
founder, non-profit Wings for Warriors

THE NINTH PRINCIPLE OF SUCCESS:
The Power of Diversification

Saturday afternoon stretched out lazily for the residents of Sunnydale, the sun mellow in the blue winter sky as Ty came out of the Copy Shop on Summer Street, bearing another hundred copies of his "Ty's Trees" flyers. He slid them carefully into his messenger bag.

Sinking down onto the bench outside, he unwrapped the sandwich he had made at home. Ty was hungry after his busy morning. He had completed his morning route, and after that it was straight to his appointed rounds: first trimming Mr. Oriole's rosebushes, then trimming Mrs. Carter's hedges, followed by raking six whole bags of leaves off Old Man Creole's front lawn.

Finally his chores were done for the day. He sighed and polished off his sandwich, washing it down with the last of the bottled water he'd brought from home. It wasn't the tastiest snack in the world, but the protein and carbs from the sandwich and the cool, fresh water were just the ticket for reviving his spirits for his next, and last, chore of the day.

"Whoa!" said Mr. Harper, frowning when Ty shuffled into Harper's Hardware Store a few minutes later. "What's going on here?"

Ty looked over his shoulder, thinking someone else must have walked in behind him. "Huh?" he asked, body weary but mind and heart racing with his recent caffeine and sugar jolt.

"You, Ty," Mr. Harper clarified. "You look like you fell into a leaf pile and forgot to dust yourself off."

As if to prove it, Mr. Harper picked half a dozen leaves out of Ty's hair and off his dirty sweatshirt. Holding them up, Mr. Harper shook his head and grinned. "See?"

"Sorry," Ty said, brushing even more off his shoulders and sides. "I've been supplementing my paper route with odd jobs on the side and…well, that's why I'm here!"

Mr. Harper winked. "I've got just the thing," he said, pointing to a large pyramid made out of leaf-bag boxes.

Ty smiled. "Well, I do need some of those, but I've got bigger fish to fry."

Mr. Harper slapped him on the shoulder and said, "That's what I like to hear, young man! How can I help you?"

"Well, here's the thing," Ty began. "I've been doing mostly lawn stuff for the last month or so. Trimming, edging, collecting leaves, cleaning out gutters, sprucing up, that kind of thing. Sometimes the person will have the tools I need on hand, in their garage, sometimes I'll have them, but then they're all the way back home, so…"

"You need a tool kit," Mr. Harper finished for him.

"A big one," Ty agreed, following him toward the back of the store. "But not too big. I still have to lug it on the back of my bike."

They paused mid-step as Mr. Harper turned to regard him carefully. "Ty, that's a tall order. I mean, are you sure you can't borrow a truck, or buy one? You're nearly eighteen, right?"

"I am, and I could, but then I'd get into car payments and insurance and gas, and I'm trying to save up for school. So I'm sticking with my bike for now."

Mr. Harper smiled his hand on the grip of a massive lawnmower. "So I guess the Grass-U-Later 6000 is out of the question, huh?"

Ty admired the massive machine. "For now," he sighed wistfully. "But I do need something for lawns when the client doesn't have their own."

"On a bike?" Mr. Harper asked.

"I could drag it, I guess," Ty said, not having thought it out this far.

"No, no," said Mr. Harper, steering him away from the lawnmowers for now. "Listen, we have these trailer hitches folks use to ride their kids behind their bikes. You've seen those?"

Ty brightened. "Oh yeah, Mrs. Madison across the street has one. She takes her twins all around town."

"Right. They're pretty sturdy," said Mr. Harper. "Well, one of my employees got the bright idea of taking one and turning it into a work trailer, like you see hitched to pickup trucks."

They stood in front of one. It was a three-wheeled cart, with a skinny wheel in the front and two wider wheels at the back. The triangular cart had three pieces of plastic fencing rising up from the bottom to create a secure-looking trailer.

"Looks sturdy enough," Ty said, wiggling one of the sides.

"It's reinforced fencing," Mr. Harper bragged. "It's welded to the cart, reinforced at the bottom and each joint, so it'll get the job done. The trick is distributing your weight and making sure you're not overloading it."

"How much will it carry?"

"Well, Ty, they're cleared for two hundred pounds, but I always suggest doing fifty pounds less than that because, remember, you've still got to lug it behind your bike."

"Good point," Ty murmured, pulling a notepad from his messenger bag. "So now I need to find out how much of my list I can fit in here."

"Don't you want to know how much it is?" asked Mr. Harper.

Ty tapped the oversized "Harper's Hardware" sticker dangling from one fence slat. "Two hundred dollars is in my budget," he said. "I was expecting to pay twice that much for a lawnmower, so maybe we can find something cheap that can fit on the trailer?"

Mr. Harper nodded and led him across the aisle to where the lawnmowers sat, with the big and mighty to the left and those dwindling in size — and price — to the right. "I think I've got your solution," he said, inching toward the end of the row. "This is our Retro Shredder model. It's propulsion powered, meaning the more you push it, the harder it works."

"Is it electric?" Ty asked, peering at the Retro Shredder. It was small enough to fit in the bike cart, at least. It featured a round cylinder at the bottom, about three times as thick as the rolling pin his mom used to make Thanksgiving pies. The cylinder was covered in shiny curved blades. A long, slender bar stretched from the cylinder housing and forked into two handles, like his bike handlebars, about waist high.

"What's it do?" Ty asked.

"Give it a try and see for yourself," Mr. Harper said, taking it off the display rack and resting the barrels on a strip of artificial turf that bordered the lawnmower display.

"Really?" Ty asked.

"Sure," said Mr. Harper, tapping the handlebars. "It's fairly simple. You grab these, line up the mowing cylinder, and *push*."

Ty nodded and did as he was told. The cylinder ran smoothly over the fake, rubber grass. Ty imagined the real thing falling like tiny green soldiers beneath the whirring blade. The machine had a heavy, sturdy construction and rolled smoothly; so smoothly he found himself at the end of the strip of artificial turf before he knew it. Pivoting easily, he turned the Retro Shredder around and headed back up the way he came.

"What do you think?" Mr. Harper asked. "Pretty smooth, huh?"

"It could work," Ty said. "I'm just wondering how well it cuts real grass."

"I have one myself, just in case my Grass-U-Later 6000 conks out, and it's great. Takes a little more elbow grease than a gas or electric model, but if you're just doing your neighbors' lawns for extra money to save up for school, it should last you long after you graduate…from college!"

Ty peeked at the price tag and was relieved to see it cost only one hundred and fifty dollars. "Will it fit on the trailer?"

"Let's find out," Mr. Harper said, wheeling the trailer over and unlatching the back gate to fold it down.

Ty rolled the Retro Shredder up the ramp produced by the back gate and into the trailer. It slid into place effortlessly, taking up most — but not all — of the pint-sized trailer.

"Perfect fit!" Mr. Harper bellowed. "And plenty of room for whatever you need on your list there." He snatched the paper out of Ty's hand, sliding reading glasses on as he squinted at it. "You know, Ty," he said, leading his eager pupil through the nursery section, "a lot of these things can be bundled to save you more room."

"Like what?" Ty asked.

"Well, here you've got both a rake and a hoe," Mr. Harper said, "but I've got the new Rake-U-Later, which comes with three detachable heads: one's a rake, one's a hoe, and you get a bonus shovel attachment."

"All with the same handle?"

"Check it out," said Mr. Harper, handing him a single handle, polished and smooth like a broomstick. One end was a typical rake with shiny metal prongs, while the other end featured a similarly sturdy hoe attachment. At the top, in a shiny bag, was a shovel attachment.

"This would be better than having three separate tools," Ty admitted.

"These hedge clippers should do the trick," Mr. Harper said, handing over a pair of giant, wood-handled shears. "It's way more precise than a gas-powered edger, and a fraction of the price."

Ty nodded, adding them to his cart.

"Match that with a tool belt," Mr. Harper said, handing over a small green apron with several pockets filled with handheld garden forks, trowels, spades, and other small tools, "and you should be able to tackle any job that comes your way."

"These wouldn't hurt," Ty said, grabbing a sturdy wheeled trashcan and several boxes of trash bags off of the pyramid display near the sales counter. "That way I could quit borrowing them from people."

"That's most of your list," Mr. Harper said, handing it back.

"What'd I miss?" Ty said, seeing that they'd ticked off every item Ty had thought of, and several he hadn't.

"Bug spray," Mr. Harper said, sliding a can next to Ty's pile atop the register counter. "You can't be a proper landscaper and not get bitten from time to time."

"I suppose you're right," Ty said, doing some mental calculations in his mind. "Thanks for all your help today. This is really going to make my life a lot easier."

"And a little less profitable," Mr. Harper said, beginning to ring up all the items. "At least for now, anyway."

"Actually," Ty said, reaching for his wallet, "now I'll be able to do twice as many jobs in half the time."

"How do you figure?"

"Well, look at today," Ty told him, finding a leaf in his wallet, of all places! "It took me twenty minutes to race back to my house and grab the rake that Old Man Creole told me he had, but didn't. Well, he did, but it was all rusted, and when I went to use it, it fell apart. Then I had to stop and get gas for Mr. Carter's trimmer, and that took nearly an hour, and that's beyond all the work I had to do after I got all my tools gathered."

"I hear you," said Mr. Harper. "But you're spending nearly $500 today."

"I'm not spending it," Ty corrected him. "I'm *investing* it."

"Fair enough," Mr. Harper agreed.

"And about that bill," Ty pressed, tapping a stack of Harper's Hardware promotional flyers on the counter next to the cash register. They were one-page brochures, split up into two columns, with four coupons on each side. "What if I were to hand a few of those out while I was doing my odd jobs around town?"

Mr. Harper turned, trying not to laugh. "Are you suggesting I give you a discount for passing out coupon flyers, Ty?"

"Well, it would be free advertising," Ty insisted. "And I'm doing work on nine different streets, with people driving by, waving, and asking what I charge. Think of all the great PR you'll get when I tell them I got my tools at Harper's Hardware *and* hand them a free flyer full of coupons with my bill!"

"You drive a hard bargain, kid," Mr. Harper said, handing Ty half the stack from beside the cash register. "But you do make a good point!"

Ty tapped the handheld calculator beside the register. "Yeah, but *how* good a point?"

"Let's see," Mr. Harper said, tapping the calculator keys. "You're looking at $500 for all the hardware and supplies you're buying today.

You've got a stack of flyers. I figure you'll probably hand them out and get some more if you think about it, or not. I'll probably make a few sales off of them, which would be great. For all of that I'll knock ten percent off your bill."

Ty nodded. It was a good deal for both of them. He could save fifty dollars today, but what about next time? "Is that a one-time-only deal?" he countered.

Mr. Harper stood back and eyed him shrewdly. "Naturally," he said.

"I only ask because I'm doing a few jobs every day, which means I'll be handing out these flyers pretty regularly. Plus, I'm not putting them under people's windshields, I'm handing them to clients face to face. That means I can point out something I think they need…" His voice trailed off.

Noticing a new trash barrel for twenty-five dollars off with the coupon only, he tapped it for emphasis. "Like this trash bin for Mr. Erickson, or the gardening gloves for Mrs. Bradley. So…"

Mr. Harper waved a hand, indicating he'd heard enough. "Tell you what I'll do, Ty," he said, speaking slowly as he no doubt ran the figures in his mind. "I'll give you a choice. You can save twenty percent off your order today, or I'll give you five percent off every purchase you make until you go away to school."

Ty frowned. "Not ten percent?"

"Five," Mr. Harper said. "Sleep on it, if you need to."

"I don't need to," Ty said. "I'll take the five percent discount, please."

Mr. Harper's face fell a little, clearly disappointed. "You sure?"

"There's no choice," Ty said. "I mean, next week I could come in for two bags of mulch, or my rake could break, or I need a tool I didn't grab today. I'd rather get five percent off next week than save a hundred dollars today."

Mr. Harper rang up the sale, good and final. "I was afraid you'd say that," he groused, taking Ty's $475.

"Don't worry," said Ty, loading the rest of his goods into his new bike trailer. "I'm going to make sure you get your money's worth starting right now."

Mr. Harper laughed. "Whaddya mean, Ty?"

"Well, I wasn't supposed to rake Mrs. Myer's leaves until tomorrow morning," he explained as Mr. Harper held the door open for him to wheel out his new bike cart. "But since there's still plenty of daylight left, and I've got my new flyers, I'm going to head straight over and start advertising for you right away."

"First things first," Mr. Harper said, and he bent to tighten the bolts that attached the bike cart to the back of Ty's frame. "I want to make sure you get there safely. Now, give it a spin around the corner and back and let me see how it works."

Ty did just that, getting off to a rocky start, as he was unused to the extra weight. But by the time he made it around the corner and back — and then once more just to show off — he realized the cart would be the perfect solution to his problems.

"One last thing," Mr. Harper said, zipping back inside and then right back out. He handed him a plastic bag full of different-sized bungee cords. "Use these to fasten the longer handles to the sides of the cart, and they'll stop rattling around so much."

"Thanks, Mr. Harper," Ty said, doing just that before tucking the extra cords into one of the pockets of his new lawn-tool belt. "And remember, if you ever need a little edging done, you know who to call!"

"Vine was incubated at Big Human; it was created there. The inspiration behind Vine is to help people create and share video on their phones. When we were working on Vine, the tools for creating and sharing video on phones were pretty terrible. We knew there was a better way."

Rus Yusupov,
co-founder of Vine

THE TENTH PRINCIPLE OF SUCCESS:
Delegating Authority

"P_{ssst!}"

Hearing the hiss through the steady drone of background noise in the crowded cafeteria, Ty lifted his head off the backpack he'd been using as a pillow and peered into the blurred face in front of him.

"Ty?"

Blinking the blur out of his eyes, Ty was surprised to see Steve Lane sitting across from him.

"Steve?" Ty asked, rubbing the sleep from his eyes. His days had been so full ever since starting the spring semester and now, with his territory ninety percent full plus "Ty's Trees" booming, he barely had a moment's peace!

He was staying up late to do his schoolwork after all his part-time landscaping jobs had been done, and getting up earlier and earlier to reach the nearly two hundred houses on his route. Lately, he'd been crashing during lunch to grab a quick forty-minute nap before starting the second half of his day.

"Yeah," Steve said, sinking down into the seat across from him. "Are you gonna eat that pizza?"

Ty groaned, shoving the uneaten slice of pizza on his plate in Steve's direction. The last thing on his mind at the moment was food. "Have at it," Ty said, sipping from his already open carton of milk instead. He didn't have much of an appetite lately, although he burned through calories like his Retro Shredder ate through grass.

"Forget your lunch money again?" Ty said. He knew Steve from the few classes they'd shared over the years. Homeroom here, gym there, and of course the few times they'd been lab partners in Mr. Johnson's chemistry class sophomore year. They didn't necessarily hang out together, but were friendly enough to say "Hey" to each other in the halls between classes.

And, apparently, share a slice of pizza together.

"Something like that," Steve said, wiping the corners of his mouth with a napkin. He nodded at Ty's backpack, smiling. "What's with all the catnaps this semester?"

Ty covered a yawn and stretched his tired arms above his head. "I've been pulling double duty ever since I got this paper route."

"Paper route?" Steve clucked, pushing the empty pizza plate away. "They still have those?"

"Yeah, I get that a lot. It's pretty sweet, though. I mean, I work a few hours in the morning and get paid like I'm working full time."

Steve sat up a little more alertly, meeting Ty's gaze. "Really?"

"Yeah." Ty yawned. "Really."

Steve gave him a dubious grin. "Well, if you only work a few hours each morning, and get paid full time, how come I see you crashing in the same corner of the cafeteria every day?"

Ty grabbed one of his handy Ty's Trees and Things flyers from his backpack and slid it across the table to Steve. "I started doing odd jobs before the holidays," he explained. "Just along my route, mostly, but folks have kept me hopping, so I do that most days after school. Between that and senior year and the paper route…"

A yawn interrupted Ty's train of thought, but Steve finished it for him: "You've only got time to sleep in the cafeteria every day!"

They both laughed. "Something like that," Ty said.

"Listen," said Steve, leaning forward as if someone might hear him in the crowded cafeteria. "You ever need any help, I mean, after school and all?"

Ty sat, frozen in place, wondering why he'd never thought of that before. "Are you serious?" he asked.

Steve nodded emphatically. "Yeah, I mean, things aren't so great at home these days. Dad got laid off at the plant and Mom's due any minute, so we could really use the extra money. I mean, I don't want to take any away from you, but if you've got more work than you can handle, maybe it'd be good for both of us."

Ty nodded. "Actually, I do." Ty scribbled his address in the border of the Ty's Trees flyer. "Meet me here after school if you're serious."

"Today?" Steve asked.

Ty grinned. "What, you're already calling in sick on your first day?" he teased.

Steve stood as the bell rang, pocketing the flyer and grinning down at Ty. "No, not at all. I just wasn't sure *you* were serious."

"As a heart attack," Ty said. "Maybe if I get some help, I can actually stay awake through lunch period for a change!"

Ty's excitement built throughout the day. He didn't want to get ahead of himself, but as the last bell rang and he leapt on his bike for home, he continued to think of how Steve might help him. Even if he did one of Ty's odd jobs every day, or every other day, he'd have an extra hour or two of time he didn't have now.

Then again, Steve could have just been full of beans. What if he worked for one day, then never again? What if he never worked at all? Either way, Ty realized he'd given him a great idea: why shouldn't Ty hire someone to help?

After all, the *Sunnydale Sentinel* had hired him to deliver their papers, and Mr. Harper hired folks to help him staff the counter at Harper's Hardware. Why should Ty do it all himself if someone was willing, and able, to help him out?

"What took you so long?" Steve teased, stepping out from the shade of the big oak tree at the end of Ty's driveway.

Ty wheeled his bike to a stop. "How'd you beat me home?"

Steve shrugged. "I just stayed on the bus a few stops longer and got off at the nearest stop."

Ty nodded, impressed. Then he asked, "You don't have a bike, do you?"

Steve shook his head. "But if the job's worth it, Ty, I can buy one."

"I'll leave that up to you," Ty said, walking his bike up the driveway toward the garage and dragging the garage door open. "But for now, you can use my extra one."

"Sweet," said Steve. "These are all your tools?"

"Pretty much," Ty explained. "Sometimes, if I need something bigger, I'll borrow it from the person I'm working for. And sometimes, if they need something really big, I'm just not the man for the job."

"Maybe with both of us, you will be."

Ty nodded. It could happen. "So, where are we headed, boss?"

"I've got two jobs on the same street," Ty said, guiding them toward Sullivan Avenue where he had a hedge-trimming job for Mr. Simons and a leaf-raking job for Mrs. Rothschild. "They're only a few houses apart, so I figure if we park the bikes in between, we can share the tools."

Steve nodded, falling in line beside Ty as they rode along.

Ty turned to him as they leaned their bikes against the tree between Mr. Simons' and Mrs. Rothschild's houses. "You want to know what you're going to get paid, don't you?" he asked.

"Wow!" Steve said. "Paperboy, high school senior, landscaper. And now mind reader? But, yeah, I just want to know if it's worth it, you know?"

Ty nodded. "Here's what I was thinking," he said. "By now, most folks pay me a flat fee for whatever I do. Like, today, I'm getting forty bucks to trim Mr. Simons' hedges and thirty to rake leaves for Mrs. Rothschild. Take your pick."

"And what?" Steve asked. "Pay you half of whatever I make?"

Ty tilted his head. He hadn't even thought of that. "No, just… whatever job you do, collect for that."

Steve looked incredulous. "But they're your jobs. You got them, and now I'm taking them from you."

Ty smiled. "You're doing me a favor," he said. "I'm tired, and I've nearly reached my savings goal for college, so at this point we're inching into 'gravy' territory. I'm still making money today, and only doing half the work, so I'm happy if you are."

"I don't know what to say, Ty," Steve said, extending a hand. "That's more than fair."

It was only once they'd gotten started working, with Steve raking leaves for Mrs. Rothschild and Ty trimming Mr. Simons' hedges, that Ty wondered if it wasn't *too* fair. After all, Steve was right: they were his jobs. And his tools. And even his bike! And yet, it seemed only fair that if Steve were doing the job, he should get paid for the work.

He'd meant what he said about his savings account: between reaching his paper-route goals a little sooner than he'd expected, and the growth of his afterschool landscaping gig, he'd been able to save far more quickly than he'd anticipated.

Of course he wasn't into giving money away, but this wasn't that.

In fact, as Ty worked, he realized now he could do even more jobs! And he could even pick and choose which ones he farmed out to Steve. And if it all worked out, they could go to Harper's Hardware and invest in another bike trailer and round of tools. After all, summer was only a few months away and they'd need all hands on deck to take on the full-time jobs waiting for them during those long, hot months.

And best of all, by giving Steve the entire fee for each job, he'd just found a way to motivate his newest employee to not only do a great job on every job, but to keep coming back for more. If Steve's family was having a hard time, an extra twenty or even forty dollars a day could really help. And on the weekends, Ty often did three or four jobs per day, so Steve could expect to double, even triple that.

"What's next, boss?" Ty looked up, clippers in mid-clip, to find Steve standing in front of him, leaves in his hair, a big grin on his face, and thirty dollars in his hand.

"You're done already?"

In reply, Steve pointed to five trash bags full of leaves lined up curbside and one very happy Mrs. Rothschild, waving to them from her front porch.

"Wow!" Ty said, waving back before turning to Steve. "Well, I'm almost done here. If you're free, I've got another job over on Tidewater

Street. It's a pretty big one — mowing Mrs. Archipelago's lawn and edging her drive — so maybe we could split it up and divide the money fifty–fifty."

Steve pocketed his money and hopped on his bike. "Sounds great!" he said, waiting for Ty to finish.

When he did, they loaded up their gear and headed off for the next house. Any misgivings Ty had had about Steve disappeared in the first few minutes they worked together, with Steve taking the harder job of mowing while Ty moved behind him to edge.

When the job was through it was almost dark out. Ty divided the sixty-dollar fee right down the middle. "You didn't have to do the hard part," he said.

Steve pocketed his second thirty dollars of the day and smiled. "Sure I did, Ty," he said. "It's the least I can do to thank you for letting me work for you."

"Correction," Ty said as they got back on their bikes and headed for home. "Work *with* me."

"Fear might always be there; you just have to learn ways to work around it. Having a partner will make things easier. Having a partner makes you feel less alone and more like you are supported. Also, a mentor and partnership are really great to have.... Or you have a friendship, and every day you share ideas back and forth for forty-five minutes. Setting up some routines that you work on every day get you into a situation where it's not so hard to start. A lot of fear is just fear of getting started."

Jonathan Feinstein,
professor of economics and management,
Yale University

THE ELEVENTH PRINCIPLE OF SUCCESS:
Branding for the Future

Ty rounded the corner after serving his last house on the block, his *Sunnydale Sentinel* bag empty and his spirits high. With only a few weeks left in his senior year, Ty had reached and exceeded his goals. He now had nearly two hundred houses on his route, signing up over ninety percent of the homes in his territory. He did pretty well just from delivering papers and, if he'd been careful, could have met his savings goals simply with his morning job.

But ever since hiring Steve, Ty's Trees had taken off! Not only could Ty do twice as many jobs every afternoon, and nearly a dozen every weekend, but also he didn't even have to hustle as hard for the jobs.

Ty hadn't realized it at the time, but when he hired Steve, he got more than a landscaper or laborer — he got a born salesperson. Steve was competitive, and because the money he was earning was going straight to help out his family, he was highly motivated.

As he worked on one job, he made sure to keep his eye open for neighbors, or even passersby. He'd linger at the end of the drive, trimming an already finished hedge, just to make sure he caught the neighbors coming home in case they wanted similar work done. He always kept a stack of flyers handy; in its redesign, Steve's cell phone number appeared as prominently as Ty's.

Ty rounded the corner to find Steve already waiting, oiling up the lawn tools in his own bike trailer.

When it was clear that they were getting more and more jobs, Ty had told Steve that if he bought his own bike, Ty would invest in a bike trailer full of tools.

Steve being Steve, he'd shown up the next day with a beat-up bike and a grin on his face. Ty being Ty, he'd kept up his end of the bargain and fitted Steve out the same way his own bike was equipped: new three-wheel bike trailer, new Retro Shredder, and a full complement of the lawn tools he'd first bought for himself.

Now Steve smiled, fresh and ready to greet another busy weekend. "How'd it go?" he asked, mouth half full of the protein bars he liked to munch on throughout the day.

"No broken windows," Ty joked, as he did every weekend.

"You know," Steve said, "you're going to need someone to take over your route when you head off to college in the fall."

Ty nodded, hitching his own work trailer to the back of his bike. "I hadn't really thought that far ahead," he confessed, tightening the bolts that affixed to either side of his bike tire. "Who do you have in mind?"

Steve grinned, making sure all his tools were in place — and would stay that way — throughout the long weekend. "You have to ask?"

"You're not going away to school?" Ty asked, already picturing what he'd hang on the walls of his dorm at the Ivy League college that had accepted him earlier that year.

Steve shrugged. "I can't afford it, and my grades aren't good enough for a scholarship, so I'm going to Sunnydale Community College for my first two years."

Ty nodded. Fall seemed so far away, and yet he'd been working toward it for the last three years!

How could he have spent all that time counting his pennies and budgeting his movie money, not even buying a car to save on gas, without thinking about whom he'd give his paper route to when he left for college?

"It's not just the route," Ty reminded Steve, nodding toward the stray flyer sticking out of the backpack he always wore to every job. "I'll need someone to take over Ty's Trees and Things, too."

Steve got on his bike. "I'm planning on taking a light load that first semester anyway," he said, waiting for Ty to ride alongside him, their tools clattering in the twin trailers behind their bikes. "So it would leave me more time to do the work."

"Yeah, but who would you hire to replace me?" Ty teased.

Spring was in the air, a hint of summer in the warmth that met them with the rising sun. "Nobody," Steve insisted. "I can do it all myself."

"That's what I thought," Ty reminded his new partner. "At least until that day you scarfed up my pizza in the cafeteria. Remember how tired I was?"

Steve shrugged. "Yeah, but I'll lose half my money if I hire someone to replace me. Won't I?"

"That's what I thought, too," Ty said. "But actually, bringing you on board has let me earn even more money."

"How so?"

"Well," Ty explained as they cruised through the quiet streets of his subdivision, "after catching up on my sleep and investing in a few new tools, I found I was able to still do two or three jobs per day after school. So I didn't lose any money even by splitting my work with you. And with you doing as many jobs—"

"Or more," Steve reminded him.

"Or more," Ty laughed. "But every job we do tends to lead to one or two more. You know how it is: you're raking leaves and somebody drives by and asks if you can do theirs as well. You hand them a flyer, and they call the next day, or the next week; so the more we're out here, the more jobs we get. With you, we get twice as many jobs because not only are you out here every day, but you're a hustler, too."

"Well," said Steve, chewing his bottom lip as if thinking up an excuse.

"Don't get me wrong," said Ty. "That's a good thing! I could make even more if I hustled, but I've got the route in the morning, so…" His voice trailed off.

Steve was watching him carefully. "So you're saying if I hire another hustler like me, we can clean up!"

"If you keep the quality up," Ty reminded him. "I mean, not you, but whoever you hire."

Steve frowned. "Yeah, I don't want some clown messing with the brand."

Ty smiled; he'd never thought of it before, but Ty's Trees *was* a brand.

They had pulled up to the park in the middle of the subdivision, where they hung out every Saturday and Sunday morning splitting up the work details for that day. Steve got off his bike, waving his hands excitedly. "I'm just saying; we've got this great name, Ty's Trees and Things, but…" Steve looked at their bike trailers, as bland and as generic as the day Ty had bought them. "Who would know it were *us* out there doing the work?"

"Well," Ty said. "I mean, we are doing the work. So all anyone has to do is look at us and—"

"No," Steve interrupted. "I mean, think ahead. Think bigger! What about next year, when you're gone, right? And I hire some new person, and they're out there trimming the hedges and mowing the lawns? Nobody will know them, right? They could just be working for Joe Blow's Trees."

Ty laughed. "So, what?" he asked. "We should work harder?"

"No," Steve said. "*Smarter.*"

When Ty looked back with a confused expression, Steve explained: "Like the way our flyers are yellow. We should get some yellow shirts and caps and stickers to put on our bikes so folks know it's us. That way, if we're inside getting a drink of water and some neighbor drives by looking for lawn people, we won't miss an opportunity. They could see the stickers and get our number that way."

Ty nodded, impressed. He thought he'd covered all the angles, buying the equipment and hooking up the trailer hitches, but Steve was right. "That's a really great idea," he said. "We should get on that…"

Even as he spoke, Steve was whipping off his backpack — fuller than usual this morning, Ty suddenly noticed — and unzipping it. From inside, he pulled out a burst of yellow and green. "We already did," Steve explained, tossing Ty a bright-yellow T-shirt.

Ty opened it up to reveal "Ty's Trees and Things" printed in green lettering on the front. The text curved above a tree in full foliage. On either side of the tree was a lawnmower, and beneath each lawnmower a phone number: one for Ty's cell, one for Steve's.

"Wow, Steve," Ty said, putting the shirt on. It was a perfect fit. "This is…whoa!" Steve tossed him a green cap, this one with yellow writing and bearing the same tree-and-lawnmowers logo.

"I wanted yellow shirts and green caps, you know?" Steve explained. "For the brand."

"These are amazing," said Ty. "I'll contact Mr. Harper about our discount deal. I'm sure he'll want to have us include his store logo on our next batch of shirts. Maybe I can get him to bump up my discount to ten percent now!"

Steve handed Ty the last of the treats from inside his backpack: yellow bumper stickers with green writing. "Now, even when we're not around the brand will still be strong," Steve said with pride as he and Ty slapped the bumper stickers on the sides of their bike trailers.

As if to prove his point, a car stopped alongside the park, a familiar face poking out the driver's side door. "What are you two hooligans doing out this early in the morning?"

Ty and Steve walked over, showing off their new shirts. "Just working on our branding, Mom," Ty said.

"Hi, Mrs. Chandler," Steve said.

"Hi, Steve," she said, smiling. "Well, your 'branding' is certainly working."

"What do you mean?" Ty asked.

"I could see your shirts from down the street!" she said, waving before she drove off, no doubt to an early-morning client meeting at the office or open house for some new property she was trying to sell.

"See?" Steve said, hopping back on his bike. "They're working already."

"Yeah." Ty chuckled, getting on his bike as well. "Too bad I already mow her lawn for free!"

"Once you come to grips with your selfish reason for being an entrepreneur, you also need to realize that you're going to need the help of a lot of people, and that means you need to be a leader. Being a leader means you need to be selfless. You have to make everyone around you feel like you will make them successful. So you ultimately you put their success on par with, if not higher than, your own success, and that makes people incredibly loyal to you and willing to dedicate their lives to you and to making your vision a success in the real world. Ultimately, that is the spirit that every entrepreneur needs to have to be successful."

Derek Lidow,
CEO, entrepreneur, professor

Applying These Principles

Ty, a high school student attempting to secure money for college, looked for employment that would fit his busy senior year schedule. He wasn't alone. As summer jobs went by the wayside and several hundred high school kids competed for the last few dozen jobs going into senior year, Ty found himself crowded out of the local part-time job market.

When he heard a disgruntled paperboy complaining about his meager route and even more meager prospects, Ty asked if his route was available — and how big it was. When he learned there were nearly two hundred households up for grabs, he leapt at the chance, seeing opportunity where the old paperboy saw only disappointment.

Though he didn't fully understand the newspaper-delivery business, Ty jumped right in because that was his only opportunity; furthermore, it would fit with his full senior year school schedule.

My own father was in a similar situation, scrambling to find a job in Boston at a young age. What he learned at the age of sixteen influenced how he would later succeed in America.

Like my father, Ty learned the Eleven Principles of Success:

The First Principle of Success: *Recognizing Opportunity*
The Second Principle of Success: *Investing in Success*
The Third Principle of Success: *Harnessing Ingenuity*
The Fourth Principle of Success: *Overcoming Objections*
The Fifth Principle of Success: *Adding Value, Reducing Costs*
The Sixth Principle of Success: *Creating Raving Fans*
The Seventh Principle of Success: *Crushing It with Consistency*
The Eighth Principle of Success: *Scaling for Growth*
The Ninth Principle of Success: *The Power of Diversification*

The Tenth Principle of Success: *Delegating Authority*
The Eleventh Principle of Success: *Branding for the Future*

By applying these eleven principles of success in any area of business, whether you are a top-flight entrepreneur launching a new startup or an underpaid paperboy, you can enhance your business through dedication, momentum, and commitment.

It may not happen overnight. It didn't for my father, and it certainly didn't for Ty. But few success stories just spring up fully formed. Instead they evolve over time, like Ty's did his senior year in high school. And he's still learning.

Who can predict what Ty might do once he gets a college degree under his belt? Then again, that's half the fun of success: discovering what the future holds even as you live it!

Q&A | ENTREPRENEURS, PROFESSORS, AND BUSINESS LEADERS

General David Petraeus

General Petraeus served in the U.S. Army and was director of the CIA.

Q: The form of leadership used in the Army is a combination of teamwork and the opportunity to lead at all levels within the hierarchical structure. How would you say that experience translates to an entrepreneurial endeavor?

A: I think that whether you are working in the military context or as a business entrepreneur, leaders have to perform certain key tasks. Those who are successful in performing those tasks will succeed overall. You have to command effectively throughout an organization. If you oversee an organization, you have to determine how it needs to be refined and updated over time, so you can repeat the process. Beyond that, leaders also need to provide the direction, energy, encouragement, inspiration, and so forth for each of those reports directly to the leader, and also for the overall organization. And the leader has to get that right as well.

Q: You have been called the warrior-scholar or the soldier-scholar. How do these traits help you now in the world of business? How important is the link between physical and mental toughness?

A: I think whether you are in government or in the world of business, leaders have to be able to analyze thoughts and information from multiple sources and determine the key conclusions from all that information, and use all that to make decisions. I found that the rigorous academic experience that I enjoyed at Princeton, including the process of researching and writing a dissertation, helped me develop these skills and helped me develop my ability to communicate.

Q: What are some habits that you had as a soldier that you still hold on to today? How important is it to cultivate good habits in order to achieve success?

A: I have a pretty reasonable work ethic and a certain degree of stamina. I've been in been in ten US cities in the last three or four months. I have an ability to synthesize and analyze lots of information, as well as interpersonal skills and an ability to communicate orally and in writing. I also have an ability to commit pretty relentlessly to a particular endeavor. Life is a competitive endeavor, and that means that sometimes you are competing to be the best team player, not just best overall. Team work is critical. But the bottom line is you really have to commit to something if you're going to be successful in it.

Q: During your thirty-seven years as an officer in the US Army, you oversaw a number of multinational combat operations, including large-scale operations in Iraq and Afghanistan. Looking back, do you see anything you would have done differently? What has been your biggest take-away from your years of being a military leader?

A: Well, sure, there are always various actions I would have done differently. Without question there were missteps and mistakes along the way. Certainly some of those were in the policy realm, such as when writing the submission for the confirmation hearing for the surge in Iraq. Again, we all have to strive to learn what motivates us, learn from our experiences, and what feels right and what feels wrong. There's a strong component over the years to having formal processes that help to identify lessons that need to be learned, and actions that need to be taken; in other words, how do you find the big idea? What needs to change; what do we sustain? I think that's very true of life and business as well.

Certainly there is a sense when you are in the military of being part of a mission larger than yourself: the purpose that imparts, and having a sense of community. And the honor of performing these duties alongside others who have raised their right hands and volunteered to serve our nation.

There is a sense of identity to those who serve in uniform. These are burdens and privileges to serving, and it was an even greater privilege to lead in such endeavors. The fact is, even in civilian life, leaders of business experience many of these same realities.

In terms of biggest lessons, they are probably that when it comes to leadership, leadership is an individual sport; one that has to be fine-tuned to each of the people that reports to you. And has to be fine-tuned to each organization collectively that you have the privilege to lead.

Q: What is the most important piece of advice you ever had someone tell you as a young cadet, or early on in your career? What advice would you give to today's youth?

A: The answer to both of those questions goes back to guidance that Gen. Jack Dowman gave me when he was a two-star commander and I was his aide. He recommended that I seek experiences that would take me out of my intellectual comfort zone, such as going to graduate school. I followed that advice and he was right about the importance of such experiences to my individual development.

Q: Were you ever a paperboy yourself?

A: I was a paperboy for two and a half years in Cornwall-on-Hudson, where I grew up. I delivered a morning paper from about the time I was eleven to thirteen years old. It was a tremendous learning experience. You had to be disciplined and you had to get up early. I had to be up by 5:30 a.m. and had to have all the newspapers on doorsteps by 6:30 a.m. I had a two-and-a-half-mile route, and this was fifty miles north of New York City, so the winters can be quite bracing. You have to interact with your customers and exercise salesmanship to get new customers. You need interpersonal relationships as you collect the subscription money. You will have an occasional opportunity to deal with dogs that were off leash. I learned a lot from it.

Q: What specific advice would you provide to people going through tough times and obstacles? How did you manage to get through the most difficult times? Does discipline have to be combined with some other inner strength?

A: Obviously, there has to be some degree of inner strength. One has to recognize that all we can do is the best we can do; we need to learn from our experiences and take responsibilities for our action and drive on.

The same thing goes for those going through stock market declines, a tough job market, or being turned down for a business loan. You have to soldier on. You have to put your head down and lean forward. Life has its tough moments. You have to recognize they're out there. The measure of the person isn't how he or she deals with success, that's easy. It's how you deal with setbacks. Life is full of them. The surge in Iraq presented daily setbacks. Really tough moments. Hard casualties. It was disheartening, frustrating, and full of maddening situations. And that could lead you to throw in the towel. But if you believe that you are pursuing the right course of action, then you need to have fortitude and have the strength to drive on. You have to keep trying to learn, keep trying to improve, keep trying to do better, and achieve your objective.

Josh Linkner

Josh Linkner is an entrepreneur, author, and speaker. He founded several companies, including ePrize, an interactive promotion agency, where he served as CEO and executive chairman. Since 2010, Linkner has served as CEO and managing partner of Detroit Venture Partners, a venture capital firm helping to rebuild urban areas through technology and entrepreneurship.

Q: In one of your YouTube video clips, you discuss the need to be a disruptor, an innovator, an artist, and an entrepreneur, and how important creativity and innovation are to having a successful business. How do today's entrepreneurs constantly keep their creative edge? Where do you draw your own inspiration and creativity from?

A: What I found over and over again is a pattern where great people and great companies are the ones that remain the most creative. The problem is, when you're a little kid or a kindergartner you're very creative, but unfortunately our schools, our system, and our jobs beat it out of us, so we become less creative as we get older, even though it's arguably the most important business skill that we need. How do we keep it going? We prioritize it. We make sure creative approaches are a priority culturally, and also how we measure things. For example, if your company says a certain percentage of its revenue will come from new products instead of old ones, now you have a corporate mandate to drive innovation.

Make sure the culture you're building, and how you treat yourself, are removing fear. It turns out fear is the biggest blocker of creativity. If you can remove fear, the more creative you will become. You can do this through a number of techniques that create a safe environment.

Lastly, look at your approach to failure. If you want to remain creative and at the forefront of industry, you're going to scrape up your knees. There's never been a professional baseball player with a 1,000 batting average. You're going to strike out. How you deal with failure is going to be impactful in how you harness creativity or suppress it. So when you deal with failure, look at it like data; like: wow, that stunk, I screwed something up, but what can I learn from that, how can I get better, how can I adapt and change? It's not so much if you fail or not — people are going to fail and have setbacks — it's how you deal with those failures. You can look at failure as an opportunity to learn and grow, or look at it as a catastrophic event.

Q: One of the commonalities that you have found among leaders and innovators is that they defy tradition. It's hard sometimes to be the one to break the mold, or go against the grain. What would you say to those people who want to innovate, but feel their efforts are unsupported or underappreciated?

A: There are always going to be people around you to tell you no. When you study history and the people who made the biggest impact in the world, they were also told no by a bunch of people and weren't supported. But they didn't let those detractors hold them back. So I would say to someone who feels like they have some ideas and wants to do something different, but others around them are not being supportive: try to surround yourself with people who are supportive, or not to let those people bring you down.

They don't write history books about people who just did what they were told or just followed tradition and didn't do anything on their own. Even though that's what your boss may want you to do, that's not living up to your full potential, that's not leaving your fingerprints on the world. When you zoom way out and think about how you want to be remembered, or how in twenty, forty, fifty years from now, or longer, when you are on your deathbed, you don't want to be filled with regret about all the things you didn't do, all the risks you didn't take. You want to be fulfilled, knowing that you pushed the boundaries, took some risks, and went out there.

If you connect deeply with your long-term vision for your life and long-term impact you want to make, and how you want to be remembered, it gives you the courage to stand up to those who want to bring you down.

Q: You advise people to try "throwing their imagination" at the challenges they face. What is the best way to do that? Is there a process you have found that will help people engage their imagination or creative processes?

A: What I meant by throwing your imagination at something is that too often in the business world when we are facing a problem, our instinct is: okay, I need to throw money at the problem, or people or bandwidth or computing power or some external resource. What I advise people to do is to pause before doing that, and see if you can try throwing your imagination at it. Come up with unorthodox ways to solve the problem. When you look at the problem, think if there is a way to flip the problem upside down: can I flip the instinctive way I would handle this problem upside down in order to find a better result? Have a willingness to step away from obvious answers and what instinct is telling you, and ask: what is my imagination telling me?

I love doing "role-storming," which is basically brainstorming on a problem, but in character. So in other words, when you say "How should I solve this tough problem for my company?" you are immediately filtering the question through your own perspective. You are thinking: if I say the wrong answer, what if I get fired? What if I look foolish in front of my boss? To remove that, and bring imagination to the surface, say to yourself: "How would Picasso solve this problem? Or how would Steve Jobs solve this problem? Or how would Oprah Winfrey solve this problem? Or how would President Obama solve this problem?"

Q: You are obviously a very passionate person when it comes to helping others fulfill their potential. You are also a very successful tech

entrepreneur, business leader, and author. What ignited the spark in you to become the person you are today?

A: Well, I think a combination of things inspired me. I had a grandmother growing up who I loved dearly, who passed about thirty years ago. When I was a young kid she would say to me: "No matter what circumstance you are in, whether you are in a classroom or a business meeting, someone has to be the best. It might as well be you." So the way I interpreted that, she pushed me to see that we all have our own potential, but you have to push yourself to be as impactful as possible, not just for your own personal rewards, but also for the ability to impact others in a positive way. So that's been my philosophy: this dual approach of fulfilling my own potential but doing it in such a way as to help others. It's funny — I've heard it said that the purpose of life is having a life with a purpose. If your purpose is to challenge yourself to accomplish more to help others to leave an impact, that's a very fulfilling way to spend your days. And that's been very fulfilling for me.

What I found is that if you chase money it rarely comes to you. But on the other hand, if you chase greatness, then money comes as a byproduct. There's a saying I like that says: money follows, it doesn't lead. In other words, go out and do the things you are passionate about that make a big impact on the world, and you will end up making more as a result of that than if you just chased the almighty dollar.

Q: Looking back, would you do anything differently in your career? Did you ever fail at something, and what important lessons did you learn from that?

A: I've had lots of failures. If you talk to the most successful people — and I've been lucky enough to speak to billionaires and meet the president of the United States — you will see that the people who win the most fail the most. It's not like these people are magical wizards and they never failed. They have failures too; but it's what you learn from it and how you deal with those failures that make people successful. If I could go back in my career, there are dozens of things I'd have done differently. But I'm pleased with where I am. I'm not worried about the past and I'm not filled with regret. But I would have made different moves. If you learn from the mistakes you make, the result will be that you become a better person and a better business leader as you move forward.

Q: What advice would you give to college students, or any aspiring entrepreneur, to successfully get into the entrepreneurial spirit?

A: The advice I give to college students is you should absolutely go for it. If you want to start your own business or work for a startup or become an artist, or whatever you want to do — go for it! I see so many people take a safe career, take a boring job at a consulting company, and then they are filled with regret years later because it never becomes easier to take a risk. All of a sudden you are married or have a kid or have a mortgage. The way I look at it is, if you are young and you take a big life risk, you win either way. Let's say you start a company and it works out — great! Go enjoy driving your Ferrari. Let's say you start a company and it collapses; the learning and experience and insight and knowledge that you gain from that process makes you far more valuable in the workforce, and ultimately a better persona with deeper character and experience. So you win if it works, and you win if it fails. You win either way. If there's ever a time to take a risk, it's when you are young. I have a son in college, and I was just telling him: now is the time to take risks.

Q: When and why did you begin ePrize, which is now the largest digital promotion agency in the world and serves seventy-four of the top hundred brands? How were you able to get there?

A: I started the company because everyone was doing the opposite. When I started it in 1999, there were hundreds of others focused on internet advertising, but promotions, which is a large category in the marketing mix, was basically dormant online. So I thought, instead of launching the 250th Internet advertising company, what if I started the first Internet promotion company? So right out of the gate, I starting taking the opposite approach, and that served us very well. When everyone was doing one thing, we did the opposite. And that allowed us to build a great company. In terms of how we built it: we used the skills I mentioned earlier — a lot of grit, tenacity, resiliency, a lot of creativity, and a lot of service mentality. And it was lot of hustle. It was very successful as a result of us taking a nontraditional approach.

Q: Do you believe there is some sort of pattern or formula to becoming a successful entrepreneur? What is the most important attribute an entrepreneur needs to be successful?

A: I don't. I think if you are looking for a guarantee you shouldn't be an entrepreneur. I think the whole point of entrepreneurship is you are doing something that has never been done before. There is a huge price we pay for certainty, and it's too high. So if you want certainty, go work at the post office, but you're never going to achieve anything of scale. When you look at people like Steve Jobs or Thomas Edison or Henry Ford, these were people who didn't have a guarantee, and the fact that they didn't have a guarantee drove them, and drove their passions, and drove their ability to work through impossible situations to achieve more. So I think if there was such a thing as a guarantee it would have hurt the entrepreneurial process rather than help it.

Heidi Gardner

Heidi Gardner is a lecturer at Harvard Law School and an expert on collaboration and leadership.

Q: Much of your current research is about peer collaboration, including studying partner-level collaboration, and looking at the benefits and costs to firms and individuals who work collaboratively. What led you down this road of research? Why is a collaborative environment so important?

A: I had experience working at McKinsey & Company, where we were working in teams. I often found that, despite our best intentions, we didn't draw out the full expertise of every person on the team, including not only the consulting team but also the clients who joined our team. I think we always did a solid, good job. But I felt like sometimes we were missing that spark that we could have had if we had drawn out the full range of knowledge. I was puzzled by how this could happen in a bunch of smart individuals, and eventually I left and pursued a PhD to study that topic.

What I discovered along the way is that, as hard as it is to get key members to contribute their utmost to a project when staffed on a team, it's even harder to get people who are peers to collaborate effectively. And there are sometimes situations where peers are working together and there's no designated leader on the team. Often peers are uncomfortable giving each other specific directions and constructive feedback, and sometimes people don't believe that there are benefits from collaborating and sharing the credit and getting other people involved, or asking for their help. So there are a whole range of potential barriers, and I've been studying this topic to understand the root causes of those barriers. That's why I'm interested in this topic.

What we find is that when people do take the leap of faith to collaborate and are open to getting other people involved in this work, they are directing and are also equally going to contribute to projects that other people are directing. There is a whole range of benefits that come not just to them personally, but to the firm and the clients. They are emanative; they are often more focused on providing truly added value, and associated with those good outcomes are financial benefits as well.

Q: What is the single most important lesson for a firm that wants to include more collaboration within its ranks? Are there any unexpected benefits to firms that foster more collaboration? Are there any pitfalls?

A: I think the most important factor that affects people's propensity to collaborate is the culture of the firm, and their beliefs about the trustworthiness of their peers. I think this would come as a surprise to many firms or organizations that believe they can engineer collaboration through incentives or other kinds of formal systems. What I find is the single biggest barrier to collaboration among high-power, high-autonomy peers is lack of trust in their colleagues. It can be lack of trust in people's competencies: Do I believe you have capability to handle this issue? Do I believe you are going to respond professionally and quickly to my clients' concerns? There can also be trust issues at interpersonal level: Do I believe you will treat me fairly? Do I believe you will give me credit where credit is due? Those kinds of trust issues can't be determined through formal systems and processes. The leaders of those firms have to think about building a culture that fosters belief in one another's trustworthiness, and part of that belief system stems from how the leaders themselves behave.

Q: One of your blog posts talks about the difference between collaboration and cross-selling, and the "Do you want fries with that?" approach that comes with trying to cross-sell services to a client. Cross-selling seems to be embedded in many organizations. Is there a good way to do this that adds value for the client and can bolster a professional relationship between firm and client?

A: I think the most important issue at hand is whether the professional has the interest of the client first and foremost in their mind when they start the discussion, or if it is a self-serving conversation. Inevitably, cross-selling will be a priority for a lot of firms. But what makes a difference in the eyes of the client is whether the client believes the professional is raising the possibility of a broader relationship or selling a wider set of services. If the client believes the professional is offering this truly as a way to solve sophisticated, complex issues that the client cares about, it will be perceived differently than if client believes the professional is raising these issues as a way to increase his or her own profit or credit.

What clients tell me is that when they find an advisor who truly has a deep understanding of their business and their situation, that's when they are willing to entertain buying additional services.

Q: Looking back on your career, what has been the defining moment that led you to the place you are now? If you could go back, would you change anything?

A: I think the defining moment for me goes way back before I started a career. It was part of my education. I went to a summer program called the Pennsylvania Governor's School for International Studies. This was a big leap for me: I was sixteen years old, and it was the first time I had spent time away from family and away from home. I grew up in Amish country in Pennsylvania; it is a closed community and people don't travel much. My interest in learning about international affairs was fairly unusual among my peers, so the idea that I would leave my family and travel across the state and spend six weeks studying international affairs — and in particular I was studying Japanese at the time — was highly unusual. Many people didn't understand why I would bother spending my summer like that when I was sixteen, but it opened so many doors and so many avenues for me; it exposed me to tremendously different ways of thinking, and to how big and diverse the world really was. It was a humbling experience because it helped me understand how little I really knew.

Q: What are the biggest mistakes that you have seen partners or firms make, and what is the best way to correct course when mistakes happen?

A: The absolutely biggest mistakes that come to mind are ethical breaches, and in particular when a professional makes the deadly mistake of putting their own interests above those of the clients. Those are very difficult to recover from. I think when there are breaches in confidence like that — when professionals are self-serving rather than client-first — the firm has to take strong action to make it clear that this is not sanctioned behavior in any regard, and be as transparent as possible; giving the individual in question due process and making sure everyone understands what happened, before people jump to conclusions. If it's clear there has been an ethical breach, they have to take swift action and be as transparent as possible about the mistakes that were made.

I think McKinsey & Company had a very well publicized instance of this when one of the partners was ultimately found guilty of trading on insider information. [McKinsey's] response was commendable in that they tried to be as transparent as they could be with rest of partnership, with clients, and with the media to some extent, and owning up to what went wrong and taking lots of remedial action to reassure clients that this was a rogue instance, and putting processes in place to reinforce ethicality, and monitoring that people were complying with expectations.

Anthony Ameen

Anthony Ameen is the founder of the nonprofit Wings for Warriors, which helps servicemen with disabilities cope when they return home.

Q: While other entrepreneurs began their career by studying business, or launching a startup out of their garage, you found inspiration after being severely wounded in an attack by the Taliban while serving in Afghanistan. Can you tell me about your experience, and how you were inspired to launch Wings for Warriors?

A: After serving in military for roughly eight years, I was deployed to Afghanistan. While I was serving there, I stepped on an IUD. The amount of pain I felt that morning was so intense; I wouldn't wish it on anyone. From that instant on, my life changed. What broke my heart more than being injured was how I was treated as a wounded veteran. I was heartbroken, lying in a hospital bed. I couldn't walk or do anything.

I was just hopeless. And in the midst of that hopelessness, I was being denied the financial and healthcare benefits that I so bravely fought for.

That broke my heart even more. I was so heartbroken, so ashamed, and I was so pissed off. I just felt like something was wrong and something needed to be done.

Q: What was the most difficult thing that you encountered during your recovery?

A: The hardest part about being injured was that I felt like I wasn't able to prove myself. I wasn't able to utilize all the training I did in the military. For six years I trained to be a hospital corpsman, and then for three and a half years I trained to be a hospital corpsman on the battlefield to save the life of a wounded Marine. During that time in recovery, I really and truly felt I needed to prove myself to my Marines and to my family. I felt belittled in a weird way; felt like I didn't live up to my expectations; felt I had to prove myself to others.

Creating Wings for Warriors helped with that. I told people that I might have helped twelve guys on the battlefield, but off the battlefield with my nonprofit organization, I've been able to help over 1,200 nationwide. Wings for Warriors not only pulled me from the dark place I once was, but it really showcases and forecasts what I'm capable of. I'm capable of doing a job and doing it well and being successful.

Q: How important are mentors to anyone aspiring to launch a nonprofit organization?

A: Just last night I was sitting on the back patio with my wife, telling her about a friend of mine — one of the most successful entrepreneurs I've ever known. He's very successful at what he does. He has been a mentor to me, and if I have any questions regarding my entrepreneurial journey, I can ask him, and he'll be brutally honest. His name is Jimmy Lee. He is a wealth-management CEO entrepreneur, but he is such a kind and kindhearted person. He's teaching me how to be a professional in other ways.

Q: What is the purpose behind Wings for Warriors?

A: There are families out there that are suffering, that are reaching out to me, that don't have the money, resources, or means to better their lives. When they call me, they say, "These are all the benefits I know of. Are there any others I can be helped with?" I list three or four more, and a month later they call and tell me, "Just so you know, I was just awarded fifteen thousand dollars from Veterans Affairs." And that makes me feel really good.

Or when a guy says: "Hey, I lost my leg in combat, but I was never awarded the fifty thousand dollars I was supposed to get." So I make a few phone calls. A while later, I get another phone call from him: "Just to let you know, I got my fifty thousand dollars. Thank you. God bless you."

I've done that for a little more than 1,200 people, and I've only been counting last few years.

Q: What are the pitfalls of starting your own nonprofit? What should you know before you launch a nonprofit?

A: When I decided to start a nonprofit, I read a book called *Nonprofit Kit for Dummies*. I launched Wings for Warriors based on that book. It has all the meat and potatoes of what to do and what not to do when you start a nonprofit. So I skimmed through the book and put it away. What I didn't realize was how much money it would take to launch a nonprofit. I put $30,000 of my own money into Wings for Warriors. I'm not saying every nonprofit will need $30,000, but I was able to project myself out there faster by using that money to help market the organization on Facebook and Twitter. Little things like that added up quickly. Lastly, I ordered a bunch of shirts, so when I was at events I would have marketing materials that people could wear, and it's a talking piece to bring up Wings for Warriors and how people can support it.

Q: What's the biggest chance you've taken to help launch your organization?

A: When I was getting ready to launch, I was told that when people land on your website, you're going to need media; you're going to need pictures and video. At the time I was watching the Carson Daly show before I'd go to bed, so I thought, "Maybe I should reach out to these NBC producers, and see if there's any chance that when Wings for Warriors launches, maybe we could be part of this show. So I literally cold called NBC and talked to people with Last Call with Carson Daly, and got on the show because Matthew McConaughey cancelled. It was the best timing in the world — just sheer luck. He had a nonprofit organization, so they were doing nonprofit week, so it just worked out. The night the segment aired we got $13,000 in online donations. It ran two other times, generating got $3,000 to $4,000 each time. But that night was an a-ha! moment. I realized I had created something that was going to be successful. That was four and a half years ago.

Derek Lidow

Derek Lidow is a veteran CEO, innovator, and entrepreneur who teaches a very popular class at Princeton University on entrepreneurial leadership.

Q: You are a global CEO, Princeton professor, innovator, startup coach, and author of *Startup Leadership*. You are also recognized as a world expert in the electronics industry, with a PhD in applied physics from Stanford. Tell me about how you went from electronics industry innovator to entrepreneur and startup coach. What ignited the spark in you to begin this venture?

A: When I was high school, I loved science. I was a science geek. Back in those days I wore a slide rule on my belt, and that's pretty geeky. I was really good at science, so when I applied for college I got into Princeton on the merits of my scientific interest. I was passionate and very precocious and I dove into research and working with professors all that I could. I published papers and did great work. I took extra classes, just because I loved it, not because I was trying to prove anything. I just thought this was the most fun thing imaginable, so who wouldn't want to take more classes? I ended up taking enough extra classes that I graduated in three years.

One of the professors I had written a paper with had recommended a professor at Stanford, and I worked for him between my second and third year. I loved that lab, and the teacher and I got along great. He invited me to come back to work for him in graduate school. So that greased the skids for me getting into Stanford for grad school. I had done such great work at Princeton that I got a prestigious fellowship, called the Hertz Fellowship, for graduate school. Again, I took as many classes as I could and I got to work for this famous, brilliant professor in applied physics at Stanford, working on the interface between optics and solids and gases and leading-edge quantum optics stuff.

One of my professors, even before classes started, called me into his office and said, "Hey, you're good with quantum mechanics. Let me tell you about this new theory I have." And he laid it out. Then he said, "Now go do that in quantum mechanics." And I did. But turned out his theory was wrong. I came back to him and showed him how it was wrong and I said, "This is how it really works." He argued about it for a couple of weeks, but ultimately he admitted that my theory was right.

So I was just a couple of weeks into graduate school, but I was well on my way to a PhD. I graduated with a PhD in two and a half years, at the ripe old age of twenty-two. At that point, I could have gone to teach at a major university, but I wanted to work in the real world. I wanted to affect people by developing new things. I was quickly recruited into the semiconductor industry during the golden age of semiconductors. During twenty-three years in that industry, I did virtually every job that could be done, and did it really well. I had a reputation for making good things happen.

Eventually I was a CEO of a large, global semiconductor industry. I was very successful. But after I had had been doing that awhile, I had ideas of things that I felt needed to be done. I felt I had been extremely successful. I decided to retire as a successful CEO and start my own business from scratch. I had an idea from my fellow CEOs about areas that were real problems. People would say, "It's a shame no one is doing anything about this." Then when I started working in this area, they said, "Hey, that's really cool that you're doing this. We can use this stuff." I had financial resources, a great reputation; everything possible was going for me. But it was still incredibly challenging.

This was during dotcom bubble bursting, 9/11 happening, Lehman Brothers collapsing — all sorts of challenges were thrown my way, but we persevered. So then a big company came and said we need to own your company. I said it's not for sale. And they said everything has a price, what would it take? I had investors, shareholders, employees. So I was compelled to put a forthright, but lucrative, offer in front of these people, who I respected highly. And they bought the company.

Princeton heard I had sold the company, and out of the blue they called me and said, "Hey, we are expanding our entrepreneurship program. Would you like to come and create some new classes for us?" So that changed my whole life in terms of being someone who is contemplative on what makes one entrepreneur successful and another not. Ultimately, I believe that the field of entrepreneurial leadership is underappreciated, and that became the focus of my research. And led to where I am now.

Q: The course you teach is on leadership, creativity, innovation, and design. Are these the most important elements for an entrepreneur to have? Which one trait in particular do you think a successful entrepreneur needs to have?

A: There are lots of different types of entrepreneurs. I don't think there's one trait that needs to be at the top of the list of absolutely every entrepreneur. There are some things that are going to be critically important. Many of those are dependent on what field you choose. You need to know your stuff or else you have nothing to offer. It's actually much easier to start a company than it is to grow the company to something that is valuable and self-sustaining. The skills that define a leader are the skills that are really essential for taking an idea and turning it into something that has impact on the world. The leadership skills are truly important to everyone. They may not be the top, most important skills to have. But leadership is right up there in top five or ten traits, always. That's something I've come to learn and respect, and something I've been able to convince more and more people that's true and should be understood by every entrepreneur.

Q: What three pieces of advice would you give to your students, or any aspiring entrepreneur, to successfully get into the entrepreneurial spirit?

A: A really important thing about being a good entrepreneur, and a good leader, is knowing yourself and why you are doing it. If you don't know that, you won't be successful and you will drive the people who are working for you crazy, because you'll seem inconsistent. What I tell my students is: to be successful and to be a real entrepreneurial leader, you need to be selfishly selfless.

You have to acknowledge your own selfishness as your reason for being an entrepreneur. Entrepreneurs are doing it for a reason, which is to make themselves feel good. That may mean earning money and being rich, or to prove something — like your father never thought you could do it — or to have total control over your life.

Once you come to grips with your selfish reason for being an entrepreneur, you also need to realize that you're going to need the help of a lot of people, and that means you need to be a leader. Being a leader means you need to be selfless. You have to make everyone around you feel like you will make them successful. So you ultimately put their success on par with, if not higher than, your own success, and that makes people incredibly loyal and willing to dedicate their lives to you and to making your vision a success in the real world. Ultimately, that is the spirit that every entrepreneur needs to have to be successful.

Q: Have you made any big mistakes in your career? How did you recover and what did you learn from that experience?

A: I was an unsuccessful entrepreneur and wasted a lot of money — mostly my own, but some of investors'. This was a business that I tried doing in the late '80s, so it was my first attempt, and I did it very naïvely. I made huge mistakes, but unfortunately my investors suffered, and all the wonderful people who came to work for me, who I had to lay off when I closed the company down. I didn't understand then what I have now come to learn now, about what makes an entrepreneur successful. I didn't apply any of that; I didn't come to grips with why I was doing this myself. And I did this in a field that I had no expertise in whatsoever, and I thought I was smart enough to learn what I needed to know really fast on the job, which turned out to be incorrect. To make matters even worse, I tried to do it as a hobby while I kept my full-time job, and hiring people to work for me. If you are going to ask people to dedicate their lives to you, you need to be spending your full time helping them be successful. I didn't live by my own tenets. I didn't know what my own tenets were back in those days. That was a big fiasco.

So what do you do to recover? You take stock of what you did wrong. You acknowledge it, and write down lessons learned: things I'm never going to do again. You go forward. You apologize to the people you hurt, and you don't do it again, and people will respect you for that.

Q: Do you believe there is some sort of pattern or formula to becoming a successful entrepreneur?

A: There are so many external things, random things that come into play. I teach a class called Creativity, Innovation, and Design. We look at a type of design problem that is technically known as a "wicked problem." Wicked problems are so complicated that no amount of work can describe all the constraints that you have to deal with. I teach that class because entrepreneurship is a wicked design problem. When you are designing a company, no amount of work can describe all the things you have to take into account to make sure your company is successful. There's no way you can know what the economy is going to do, or what your competition is going to do, or maybe your key partner who is your technical guru gets sick or falls in love. These are things you can't forecast or foresee.

Niko Bonastsos

Niko Bonastsos is a Principal at General Catalyst Partners, where he focuses on investments in IT (mobile, education technology, IT business applications, and consumer health) as well as seed-stage opportunities with an outlier potential. He has been closely involved with the firm's investments in Listia, Snapchat, and TuneIn, and is a board observer for PumpUp.

Q: Where did your interest in working with early-stage startups come from? You are particularly interested in working with first-time tech founders, especially those that are disruptive. What ignited in you the spark to focus in this area?

A: I always truly enjoyed working with individuals who are super passionate about pursuing a specific idea. People who all they can do is think about solving a problem their own way 24/7. This ignited in me an interest in working with startups and founders, and combined with the background I had in engineering and technology, I can apply all this knowledge and find these super-talented individuals who have the drive and have the hunger to change the world their own way.

In terms of first-time founders, I like to work with them because they don't have any legacy. People talk about the importance of experience and, in my opinion, for consumer products, experience may be overrated. Sometimes it's better when you're a first-time founder and you don't know any better. When you don't know any better, you tend to innovate a lot out of necessity or lack of experience. You learn from your mistakes. You don't have a legacy that holds you back.

Q: What advice do you have for founders who are trying to raise funds for a technology startup? As a venture capitalist who has backed such startups, what is the best pitch that you have heard from someone approaching you for support?

A: My advice for tech founders who want to raise capital is to really do your homework. And understand more about the individuals in the firms who are looking to invest in your space; what are their prior track records and what's their style? So really do your homework.

Most importantly, they should ask themselves, "Do we really need to raise capital; are we a venture-backable business? If someone feels strongly that this is going to be a five- to ten-year journey, and I'm in it for the long run, it may make sense to raise funding. If you're someone who would like to build a lifestyle business or build something that you would sell in a couple of years, it may not a good idea to raise venture capital.

In terms of the best pitch that I've heard: I remember the first time the CEO of Stripe came in here. He basically walked into the room, and said to us, "We're building Stripe. We are going to focus on enabling a new world of commerce to accept credit-card payments only." Most people in the room were like, that doesn't sound like a great idea, especially since there is such a huge amount of retailers out there.

But the guy articulated so well how quickly all these new online ecommerce businesses could be built, and how over time you would build them up with these businesses, and then you could ride the wave alongside them. This pitch was four years ago, and he killed it. Since then all the customers he signed up are now running multi-billion-dollar businesses. It's really impressive.

Q: What would say are the key elements for starting and running a successful tech startup?

A: Being an individual who loves learning, and also loves learning quickly. Because it doesn't matter what your initial idea is, and it doesn't matter who your cofounder is, if that person is learning quickly about how to work with other people, how to recruit other people, how to test your hypothesis about your idea, how to get more feedback from more users or more customers, over time that person is going to become an expert in all these different areas.

One thing that you have to remember when you're starting a company: there are going to be tons of ups and downs. You have to remember why you're in it. And how to keep going.

Q: In one of your recent blog posts, you talk about your favorite "fail tales" such as MySpace, AOL, and BlackBerry. How important is it to fail sometimes? What important lessons does failing teach us?

A: It's important to fail because that's how you learn. It's important to fail quickly because that's how you get your time back. And it's important to learn from the mistakes of others, their failures. For example, for tactical stuff, like how to figure out how to do SEO and SEM advertising, or how to figure out recruiting. Tons of people have failed on both those fronts, and you can learn from other people's experiences and their mistakes.

Q: What is the best way to tap into your creative processes? Do you have any advice on how to come up with a million- or billion-dollar idea for a startup?

A: I'll give the advice I was given myself, first and foremost. The biggest opportunities arise when there is massive change going on, like when a new hardware platform comes into play, like a new iPhone, or a new connectivity comes into play. Or some kind of technology that is much cheaper, or new legislation, like what's happening with healthcare and Obamacare.

The best founders are individuals who are always on the lookout for big changes on the horizon. And at the same time they are also looking to solve problems for themselves. They are very resourceful individuals who observe the processes they have to go through.

In terms of having a billion-dollar company, it depends on timing — you have to get the timing right. There are individuals who are brilliant and build amazing products but the market didn't open up quickly. And then there are individuals whose products are terrible, but there is such a strong market pull that everybody thinks they are geniuses.

Q: What advice can you give to entrepreneurs who want to keep pushing the boundaries, but are worried they will go too far? Can you ever be too innovative?

A: You can be too innovative, especially for strong technical founders, or someone who pushes the boundaries of technology. If you like to be kind, or use storytelling, or you can empathize with customers, you can never be too innovative; you can be ahead of your time.

You need to be in sync with users and customers. You need to see how they perceive your product, see how they talk about it, and see how it trends. Silicon Valley people often come up with complex products that are hard to explain. Those products hardly ever go mainstream.

David Perry

David Perry has created more than twenty video games, including numerous best sellers. He was founder and CEO of Shiny Entertainment. He is also the cofounder and CEO of Gaikai at Sony Computer Entertainment America, LLC.

Q: What ignited the spark in you to start a new business venture or to make significant changes in an existing business? How did the idea for your business come about?

A: My filter for new business ideas is commonly: "What would happen if you removed the friction?" Friction is any second/minute/hour of time that you feel is wasted. When you discover a better way to do something that also saves you time, it's very valuable. You could blog; then Twitter showed up and made blogging much easier for the writer and reader — that's an example. Our idea was: "What if all video games were available on every device instantly?" How could that be possible? What would we need to invent?

Q: If you had the chance to start your career over again, what would you do differently?

A: I didn't pay enough attention in school and college, and saw it just as generic "education." I wish I'd not been so lazy. I remember them asking: "Want to learn the piano?" And instead of "Of course!" I'd say, "Is there homework?" What I've learned is the more you experience things the more you can break the ice with people you meet.

Imagine you're at an event and you meet someone whose passion is piano. You think: "Damn, I wish I had taken that class!" So now, when I'm faced with a choice, I ask myself: "Will I learn or experience something new?" Then I have to do it. It's fun and the knowledge you grow over twenty or thirty years makes breaking the ice with potential business partners much easier.

Q: What are some of the biggest mistakes you've made? And how has that reflected on your career?

A: My biggest career mistake was that I worried about the transition to digital 3D, as my entire company was focused on 2D (drawing game graphics with pencils). Instead of betting on the talent we had, I sold the company, completely underestimating who was there. It was a critical business error. I did it all wrong and you can be certain I learned from it.

Q: How far are you willing to go to succeed?

A: It's just a case of "strap on the seatbelt, this is going to be a bumpy ride." It's usually a thrilling, challenging ride. I've sold companies three times now and nothing is ever "easy." It's hard, hard work.

Q: Did mentors play a role in your success?

A: Yes, I've had some great mentors over the years. One technical: Andy Laurie (UK), who was my boss and would have answers to any technical question you had. So you couldn't make any excuses as he always had answers. One business: Fred Fierst (USA) — he's done so many deals and manages to remain friends even on very tough, challenging negotiations. He's given me great advice over the years and I quote him often.

Q: Do you believe there is some sort of pattern or formula to becoming a successful entrepreneur?

A: I've seen successful entrepreneurs described as needing passion, charisma (to inspire and lead), and the ability to keep the boat pointed to its ultimate destination no matter how rough the seas get.

William Kerr

William Kerr is a professor at Harvard Business School. He is the faculty chair of the Launching New Ventures program for executive education. He focuses on how companies and economies explore new opportunities and generate growth.

Q: You are the faculty chair of Harvard Business School's Launching New Ventures program, and you also recently created an MBA course entitled Launching Global Ventures. What are the unique difficulties for a startup entrepreneur versus an established corporation when launching global ventures?

A: I think there are challenges on both sides. With a startup company, there can be challenges with trying to resolve uncertainty about a business model and difficulties in acquiring all the resources necessary, or having the ability to access resources early on. It can be very expensive early on. So you need to be able to effectively understand how to experiment, and come up with the best instant risk and reward possible and build your team up.

There are two types of core aspects in globalization. Some companies will attempt to globalize their reach through platforms like Facebook or Internet ecommerce. Others will try to have physical operations in multiple countries. Those physical operations can be a challenge to conduct because, during the startup phase, oftentimes everyone wants to be in the same room.

There is a lot of tacit knowledge and a lot of trying to figure out how to make this work. That becomes harder when people are spread across multiple countries. Typically, we find that business models for global ventures look fantastic when taking, say, manufacturing from China and resource and development from Israel or India and sales and marketing from the United States. So why would this not work perfectly? The struggle is making this operationally active and efficient, and overcoming early liability issues.

Larger companies may have a set of struggles that looks different. They can be more challenging than for a startup, or it may be less challenging for them. Large companies often have a blessing of resources. But there can be a challenge for new ventures within those large companies to access those resources. Moreover, once you access those resources, you may not be able to break those resources free from other constraints of the organization. Many large companies evaluate quarterly performance results, so they are looking at: "Are we hitting all the profit milestones and sales and growth milestones?" That may not be something that a new venture can immediately support, and it may come under pressure from the larger company environment.

In larger companies, the resources are shared, so you may have some employees, who are asked to work on a new venture, but they still have responsibilities to the larger organization, and it's difficult for them to break free.

New ventures, both small and large, need to be thought through and need a lot of effort and resources behind them to be successful.

Q: Your research focuses on entrepreneurship and innovation, including the role of immigrant scientists and entrepreneurs. What is the most important or most profound impact that immigrant entrepreneurs have on the global diffusion of new innovations and ideas?

A: Imagine throwing a rock into a pond, and there are concentric rings rippling out from where the rock impacted. A lot of the ways we traditionally have thought about technology infusion have been that type of format, so there is a mitigating factor of geographic distance. And once we have an innovation happen, the places that are closest to that source of innovation will get the idea first, and then it infuses to the next place, until eventually there are global infusions.

What we have begun to realize is that immigrant entrepreneurs and scientists are more broadly connected through global networks and professional networks. That helps us understand that innovations can grow faster between certain counties and cities based on these networks than what business models suggest. So if we have a new innovation in Silicon Valley, it may end up more quickly in Taiwan than in Japan if there is a stronger connection between Taiwan and Silicon Valley than between Japan and Silicon Valley. Likewise, it would end up in both those places more quickly than in Mexico City, even though Mexico City is much closer.

Q: What are the most common mistakes that you see MBAs make when launching startups?

A: One typical thing that we see with MBA students is that they underestimate how long it will take, and how much work will be required. So any time we see a cost projection for the early phase of a company, you want to tell them to almost double it. Or when they tell you it's going to be launched in a year, you want to tell them it's going to take two years. I think people doing new-venture forecasting greatly underestimate the difficulties in store, and how quickly time is going to pass.

Another thing startup MBAs, as well as larger companies, often under-appreciate is the importance of the core dynamics and getting everything right from an internal perspective. This includes everything from the roles and responsibilities everyone has, to the relationship with the board you create.

Most startup companies think you make it or break it based on the product market and whether you outsell someone else, or if you have the latest and greatest technology behind it. I find that as many companies fail for internal reasons and core team dynamics as do because of external market pressures and issues. That's something that needs to be highlighted for young entrepreneurs.

Third, I often counsel people to really understand if and how their business model creates customer need. You need to know if you're going to be able to fulfill good economics per products sold, and if the overall business model is successful. A lot of the business plans that don't work get created around settings where people are dissatisfied with status quo. They really don't like having to pay fifteen percent to a distributor in order to get the product from the manufacturer to the retail outlet. But they don't understand that just being unhappy with the status quo doesn't mean you can rip the distributor out of the model and make it work. You have to make sure the model that you create has viability, so that every time you sell a product, you know how much money you are bringing in, and what the cost and scale is. It's more about "How do I make money out of this?" rather than "I wish the world in this area were different."

Q: How does an aspiring entrepreneur get beyond the fear of starting their own venture? When should you listen to your fear?

A: I think listening to your fear is a reasonable starting point. You have to consider the risk you are taking. One of the things we have learned from the world's best entrepreneurs is that they hate risk. They live in an environment that requires them to handle a lot of risk and uncertainty, but they are constantly trying to figure out how to change that, or shift it off to other people, and ultimately how to minimize their own risk.

Q: What is the right balance to strike between having talent, education, and business savvy when you are an entrepreneur? How important are these three things to a business venture?

A: Well, it would be nice to have all three! I suppose in some settings, having business savvy may make you too aware, too locked in to the mindset: "This is how we do things." That's why sometimes we see the most disruptive processes come from people who have more talent, and some education and some engrained business savvy, but they don't really have respect or appreciation for how things are traditionally done.

Q: What if the thing you're passionate about is already being done?

A: There are a variety of different markets out there. Some are what we think of as "winner take all" markets, and that kind of setting can be difficult for new ventures. It all comes down to what your motivation or goal is to becoming an entrepreneur. Some want to be their own boss and focus on an area where you get to run your own business. Others want to become very rich at what they're doing, and they want to target their setting or environment to create a monopoly. They want to be the only one that can provide or sell a product or service. That creates different dynamics for how you think about others being out there.

Once you are in a global setting, you have the ability to replicate and adapt things across many different environments and there are many different opportunities out there. Maybe someone else had the idea — that's great — but now you can think about how to replicate that in Nigeria or to take it to Paris.

Q: How do you advise people to keep motivated and believe in what they're doing? Would you advise an entrepreneur to stop their venture if it doesn't seem to be working?

A: The vast majority of ventures are going to have more struggles than what the founders think they will have. Startup companies often start with the grandest of visions of how things will work out, and then it's a challenge to execute against that. Ideally an entrepreneur has a supportive network of immediate family and friends. If they are married, they have an understanding spouse, and friends to support them. But founders should also think about trying to link into the local startup community and find groups of other entrepreneurs to meet with, to be able to network with people who are facing similar challenges.

In terms of advising someone to stop if their venture isn't working, the bottom line is you can't go forever without making money. No, you don't want to think of bailing at the first sign of a challenge. That's when you need to think about adjusting your business model, and doing things that help you persist until you get this thing to work.

But you also need to keep in mind that many startup companies are not going to work. You also need to understand that ventures could have great ideas that don't work. Where we see real damage done to people's careers is if they want to throw one last Hail Mary pass, and give it one last shot, instead of realizing "This isn't working, how can we return some money to investors?" Or, "What can we learn from this as we shut it down?"

Q: How does a new startup find investors or the needed funds to launch?

A: There are many different types of ventures, and there's a range of financial options out there. Usually one of the leading indicators is how have others around you, with ventures closest to yours, found the funds to support themselves?

There's no real way to judge if a new venture will work. But you need to go in and be able to show that you did the homework. To be able to say: "I'm ready to go after this. I've looked at the people involved and the opportunities that exist." You have to show the context for your business model and framework, and that you have thought through all the pieces. To say in each category: "According to the best available evidence, it's a go."

Robert P. Miles

Robert P. Miles is a serial entrepreneur, author, educator, and professional speaker.

Q: What ignited the spark in you to start a new business venture or to make significant changes in an existing business?

A: My entrepreneurship skills were likely part of my DNA and developed early during my high school years. Like most young male school-age children, I played most team sports. I excelled at ice hockey but suffered too many concussions, so I had to find another interest. Fortunately, by the age of fifteen, I discovered high school politics and event planning. I organized charter-bus afterschool tours, movie days, dances, and assorted other events to raise money for my school.

Q: How did the idea for your business come about?

A: My teenage event planning came naturally to me since I had a captured audience of classmates that wanted to socialize after school.

Q: To what do you most attribute your success?

A: Starting early by assuming the risk of an enterprise is key.
The earlier you start the lower your risk. Also, ignorance is bliss because if you knew what it would take to be successful you might not even try.

Q: What would you say are the five key elements for starting and running a successful business?

A: (1) Ambition and desire to be successful, free, and/or financially independent. (2) Start early to enjoy less risk and greater simplicity (e.g., look at all of the successful businesses started in a garage). (3) Find a mentor

— preferably someone already in the same line of business. (4) Live way below your means so you can plow excess money back into developing the business. (5) Find the right employees, because without them growing is impossible.

Q: What three pieces of advice would you give to college students, or any aspiring entrepreneur, to successfully get into the entrepreneurial spirit?

A: (1) Find the intersection of your passion with your skill set (StrengthsFinder.com offers a simple online assessment of your strengths). (2) Get started (there are exceptions, but starting a business early is one of the most common benchmarks of successful entrepreneurs). (3) Find a mentor to guide you (preferably someone in the same line of business, who is older and willing to share expertise, strategy, and wisdom).

Q: If you had the chance to start your career over again, what would you do differently?

A: Obviously I would avoid mistakes along the way, but that being said, mistakes are the great lessons an entrepreneur needs to learn.

Q: To whom, or what, do you most attribute your success?

A: I was fortunate to be born a white male in the USA with an excellent private elementary and secondary education. I was also born with ambition, desire, and the talent for taking on the risk of an enterprise. Developing a business and becoming financially independent was the crossroads of my passion (ambition and desire) and talent. In that way I think entrepreneurs are born instead of being made. Selecting the right heroes (living or dead) early in life is also critical, since they ultimately determine what kind of person you will become.

Q: **What are some of the biggest mistakes you've made? And how have those reflected on your career?**

A: Early business mistakes were expanding into areas I didn't understand (also known as making money in the business you know and losing it in the business you don't know); hiring the wrong people (hiring employees is easy; however, managing them and firing them is difficult); and growing too fast (beyond your employees and financial resources).

Q: **To what extent are you willing to go to succeed?**

A: I placed all of my efforts and resources on the line to develop a business, so I was willing to lose everything — including my reputation.

Q: **Did you ever make a big mistake and, if so, how did you recover from it?**

A: Every successful person and enterprise has their fair share of mistakes. Mistakes are important part of learning about yourself and your business. They help you focus and often humble you. The best way to recover is to admit them, step back and learn from them, and get right back to business with your next plan or strategy.

Q: **Do you believe there is some sort of pattern or formula to becoming a successful entrepreneur?**

A: I think entrepreneurs, like athletes, leaders, and artists, are born not made. They can be molded and guided to achieve beyond their dreams, but the desire, passion, and raw talent need to be part of their DNA. That said, there are many pathways to business success, along with many formulas. The best way is to start with a good education and then go for it. You don't have much to lose when you're young.

Jonathan Feinstein

Jonathan Feinstein is a professor of economics and management at Yale University.

Q: You lecture regularly on how to foster creative development in the classroom and how to unleash students' creativity through independent student-directed projects. What do you see as the future for how students learn and how they focus their creative energy?

A: I teach a little differently from most professors. I've been teaching a class on creativity for coming up on twenty years. I have students from all over Yale University. It's been a popular class. I have undergraduates, law students, engineering students, medical students, art students. I've learned a lot, and gradually I've worked out the best way to teach the things that I want to teach.

In class and out of class, work together. But I wouldn't say that I divide things up. We do some presentation of material. I talk about different theories and approaches to creativity, including ideas from more psychological or business-oriented approaches. Using visuals and having a big screen in front of students, especially with artists, they are able to visualize it better and ask more questions, and I think it's useful. We have a lot of activities going on in the classroom. We do have some group activities going on, and doing it in the classroom is great: they are right there, and it is quality time, so you can do a lot with that.

If you're doing a group activity, whether it's a larger group like five, six, or eight people, or just a pairing, it's nice to use that time in class to get them doing something, even if don't complete it. That way they get into the flow. Then, when they are out of class, they can continue to work. I do a lot with putting students into pairs. We have students write down a creative interest they have. It's interesting to have them in pairs and to have them share with each other what their creative interests are. And then have them talk about what they just told each other, like: "How do I feel about

131

our statement of creative interest? How would I ask you questions about it to help you go further?" So I think pairing up has turned out to be really powerful.

Q: You are the author of *The Nature of Creative Development*, **which presents a way to better understand the creative process by analyzing how creative people operate and how they come to their distinct interests. What is your best advice for an entrepreneur to hone his or her creativity, or the creativity of those around them? Conversely, what are the pitfalls for those who have creative minds? What difficulties do they encounter?**

A: When people think about creativity, the first image that comes to mind is a light bulb that just turns on, and bam! That is true — people will suddenly have an idea; that does happen. But we need to step back and understand that that happens within a much longer term, richer process that they are going through. They set themselves up to have that moment. It's a long-term unfolding process that people are going through to be creative. The great moments can happen, and it's great to hear about those moments, but you have to see it in the context of their life, and what they went through to get to that point. A lot of times when I lecture about creativity, that's where I start. A lot of people don't really get that.

This process would be just as true for entrepreneurs, or even doubly so for entrepreneurs. Sure, you might have a great moment when have an idea for a company, but you had years of work before that, and frankly you have years of work after that as you refine an idea for a company. That could take a couple of years or five years to work out, and understand what you have to do to get the idea to work. You have to understand it is a process. You have to stay with the process and let it wander around, and not panic if you don't have the idea first thing in the morning when you wake up. You have to listen to yourself. It's important to be in contact with what you feel.

Q: How does an aspiring entrepreneur get beyond their fear of starting their own venture? Does fear stifle creativity, and if so how can one mitigate it?

A: Fear can stifle creativity because it prevents people from exploring their own ideas. It's not about mitigating fear, it's about managing fear. It's like what people say about being brave: it's not the fact that you don't have fear; it's that you're able to act anyway.

Fear might always be there; you just have to learn ways to work around it. Having a partner will make things easier. Having a partner makes you feel less alone and more like you are supported. Also, a mentor and partnership are really great to have. And having habits is really important. Julia Cameron, in her book *The Artist's Way*, talks about writers, and how writing is a hard thing to do. Often writers talk about the blank page and how hard that is to face. A habit where every day you spend an hour thinking about your ideas, or just writing down ideas for a half hour in a notebook in a café every day, is a great proactive habit. Or you have a friendship, and every day you share ideas back and forth for forty-five minutes. Setting up some routines that you work on every day get you into a situation where it's not so hard to start. A lot of fear is just fear of getting started.

There are other ways to manage it. I believe in a holistic life, a balanced life, including exercise, and doing all the things that help you create some balance, and so you have some confidence in your own life path. That will help you manage the fear. You can't be afraid to fail. People fail all the time — you can learn from that. You have to accept you might fail. The first failure can be hard for someone. If you don't have support, you need to look for support in whatever way you can.

Q: Do you think the idea is just as important as running your company? Before starting your company, what's more important: having the right idea, or having the right management to run the company and put your idea into action?

A: One thing I talk about with creativity is one of the most common mistakes that a novice will make. They get their first idea, and that idea is sacred to them — it's set in stone. They think: "This is my idea, so this is the way I'm doing the business, this is the way I'm writing the book. I'm not going to change."

One of the keys to becoming more experienced and more successful with any type of work is to be flexible and make revisions and learn to listen to other people and adapt, and let the idea move around. It's about finding the sweet spot. People think the first idea is super important, and it's true that that idea gets you going on the path, but it's not necessarily the idea that's going to hit the sweet spot. So I think that management is important, because management in that context really means learning to make modifications and learning to adapt and change things around until we find the sweet spot where it's going to work. I do think that's very important.

Q: What if the thing you're passionate about is already being done? How important is it to find a niche market?

A: My perspective is there is always a way to see something where it hasn't been done exactly that way. When you're twenty thousand feet above the surface of the earth, you look down and say: "Well, someone already did that; Amazon already started Internet marketing." That's true. But when you come down farther and say: "Well, my particular interest is in these kinds of products," and you think about your unique talents, and where you live and the people you know, you're going to find a niche that hasn't been developed yet. And really it's just a question of keeping on looking until you find that place. So I would never say that what you want to do has been done before. I would say: if something has been done, recognize that, and keep going with your own passion and moving your idea around, and twisting it around until you find an angle that's going to work.

Q: How do you advise people to keep up the energy to believe in what they're doing? Would you advise an entrepreneur to stop their venture if it doesn't seem to be working?

A: The biggest thing is people give up because they didn't find a way to connect their passion with a productive business venture, but really they just needed to keep working longer, keep talking to more people, move around more, and let that path wind out, and eventually they would have found that connection. A lot of it is being willing to follow the winding path and listen to yourself and look at the field, until you find the niche that's going to work for you. A lot of it is having the willingness to stay with it. If you look at successful writers or scientists or entrepreneurs, the distinguishing feature is they really worked for years to hone themselves until they had that perspective that worked for them. It's usually not very fast. Sometimes it is.

Here's a story I tell about Jack Dorsey. Jack Dorsey had these ideas as a teenager growing up in Saint Louis about sending messages, but it wasn't until ten years later when he was in San Francisco that he found a way to connect that idea with the growing internet mobile phone idea. He came up with an idea that became a productive idea for Twitter. It's an interesting story about a guy at the front edge there. Most people would never have guessed this is the way this story unfolded, because you look at Twitter and think, wow, it's so simple, didn't he go home one weekend and figure it out? That is so far from the truth. It goes back much further than that.

Rus Yusupov

Rus Yusupov is a cofounder of Vine and Big Human, and currently serves as Vine's creative director.

Q: Where did you find the inspiration to cofound Vine and Big Human? These are two pretty different ideas. What is the genesis story for each?

A: Big Human is a design and engineering studio founded in 2008. It was really founded to help friends of mine who were creative, and to create a team of super-creative and talented folks to build new services and new projects for friends and clients, and also for ourselves. Big Human is part services business, and also an incubator of products.

Vine was incubated at Big Human; it was created there. The inspiration behind Vine is to help people create and share video on their phones. When we were working on Vine, the tools for creating and sharing video on phones were pretty terrible. We knew there was a better way.

Q: You consistently focus on being original and unique and different from the rest. In your opinion, are things that are new or original generally better than things that are old? What about putting a new spin on an old idea? And when does an old idea become new again?

A: I think what's really incredible about modern technology is that it has enabled a new generation of creative activity and creators.

I was a creative kid. I've been drawing and painting since I could grip a crayon in my hand. And that influenced me as I was growing up. Nowadays we have the power to create in richer and richer ways. We come from a world where we share our thoughts in a text of 140 characters, or a Facebook status update.

We are also living in a world where photos are the predominant way we are creating and sharing. But we are going through a transition where video creation is becoming even more important than photos. I think expression and creativity is an innate human characteristic and technology, and creator tools are enabling new forms of creation.

So Vine is both an old thing and a new thing at the same time. The format, the six-second square looping video — that technology is new. But people are using Vine to tell stories. People have always told stories; I don't think that's ever going away.

Q: To what do you most attribute your success? What would say are the key elements for starting and running a successful and unique business?

A: Really just having a focus on and hunger for creating new creator tools, and creating ways for people to create. I look back on examples such as Beethoven; if it wasn't for the person who created the piano, Beethoven wouldn't have been able to do what he did. So it's a drive to create new things. And you have to have a strong entrepreneurial sense.

Also, maybe it's the fact that I'm an immigrant. I wasn't born here in the US — I emigrated from the former USSR. I saw entrepreneurship as my calling, and specifically inventing new things and tinkering and so on.

In terms of key elements to starting and running a successful business: I think that focus is important. Being committed to doing one thing, or solving one thing. I think it's important to find incredible people to work with. I think it's a skill to identify talent. Talent is really important. And also being real and understanding what you've created and how it is important. Also being able to hyper-focus on things that aren't working.

Also, I think it's important to be able to identify the right time to introduce something new. Something may not have worked ten years ago, but it may work now. So: being able to see when it's the right time to put together something and seeing the right product–market fit.

Q: You are an adjunct professor at New York University of Continuing Professional Studies. What three pieces of advice would you give to your students, or any aspiring entrepreneur, to successfully get into the entrepreneurial spirit?

A: Number one: Have a problem you are trying to solve.

Number two: Find the right people to work with. If you are building a technology platform, you'd better have a background in technology or be connected to someone with a technology background.

And number three: Be prepared to fail. Be prepared to focus on something else. At the end of the day, invention and entrepreneurship should be what drive you, not a specific solution to the problem.

Q: If you had the chance to start your career over again, what would you do differently?

A: I would have had more of the conversations that I neglected to have. Often entrepreneurs find themselves in a tough position, where they need to break some news or deliver some info. They become shy or self-conscious or anxious about having those conversations. Looking back, I would be more bold and courageous in having those tough conversations. As long as you are sure it's the right way to go, I would advise you to give it to people straight. I would have been more open to communication, for sure.

Also, I think working with friends is a mistake a lot of people make.

Q: What are some of the biggest mistakes you've made? How did you recover from it?

A: I once hired a friend, who unfortunately didn't grow with the company. I had to part ways with him, and it ruined the relationship. But I did reach out afterward and call him back and now we are friends again. We both understand that that was a mistake.

Q: To what extent are you willing to go to succeed?

A: I think I would make myself uncomfortable for a little while. Entrepreneurship is about putting in the work at the beginning to achieve a dream, and seeing it pay off in the long run. So I wouldn't hurt myself, but being a little uncomfortable for a little while is definitely something I would do.

Where do I draw the line? I think it's at family. If I find my personal life and family life are being disturbed because of an entrepreneurial dream that I'm taking a chance on, I know I'm doing something wrong. I believe a good balance between solving the problems of the world and being fulfilled and happy is really important.

Robert Chess

Robert Chess is a serial entrepreneur in the life sciences field and a lecturer at the Stanford Graduate School of Business. He is currently actively involved in the running of several biotech companies.

Q: Your focus is in science-based industries, such as biotech, clean tech, and information technology. How do you foresee these fields changing over time? Are there any major developments that you hope to see in the near future?

A: I'll focus on healthcare. There's almost a sea change going on in the healthcare industry right now around what I will call precision healthcare, which is taking a patient-centric point of view as to how health and medicines are developed, rather than the old one-size-fits all model. What I mean by that: if you looked how drugs used to be developed, you would go out into nature or into the rainforest and come back with samples of dirt, would try and scour it and see if there's anything interesting that could potentially be a medicine. It's almost like the old saying, if you put enough monkeys and enough typewriters together, you'll eventually get the Bible. It was almost that approach to medicine. It was: let's test everything out there and maybe we'll find something that looks interesting.

Nowadays there's a better understanding of the genetic composition of disease and the genetic composition of individuals. We even look even at the bacteria communities that live within individuals, and use those to develop new medicines that are tailored to a specific mechanism in that particular disease, and we're also looking at the profiles of individuals and their particular disease and using that as a basis for selecting what drugs or interventions will work on them.

Q: Science-based tech and biotech are two of the areas that you are focused on. What are some of the unique challenges to launching startups in this field?

A: Often the amount of capital you need to raise is really high, in contrast with the information you have probably seen in *The Lean Startup* — which is a really good read by Eric Ries. But a lot of that stuff [in *The Lean Startup*] isn't applicable in science-based business. You can be doing the science technology for three years, five years, or eight years, and may need to raise tens of millions, or in some cases hundreds of millions of dollars before you know if your product works, or if your technology works or doesn't work.

For a lot of tech startups you are running a sprint race; for science-based entrepreneurship it is more of a marathon. You need to manage your teams because, in a marathon, you need to keep them together for a long time. You need to raise lots of money and keep investors focused for a long time and be able to show progress points along the way, and you'll need to take big bets because you can't test out if you are right for a long period of time. So you're taking a lot of personal risk because you can spend five to seven years working on something, and then find out it doesn't work.

Q: Your teaching focuses on exposing students to complex, real-world issues and trade-offs. What is the most important lesson you want them to learn while they are in your classroom?

A: I think two things are most important. Number one relates to what we talked about earlier. This is about doing something that really matters to society; it takes about the same amount of work as doing something that doesn't really matter. So you might as well focus on something that does matter. You can do just as well, and you'll feel a lot better about what you're doing, and over the long term you will make a bigger difference. That's one underlying theme.

A second one: things are very complex and you need to look at them from many directions. As an entrepreneur you need to divide your brain into two halves. The first half is the optimistic visionary half; you see what the long-term goal is, you keep focused and motivate others and stay positive about what you can accomplish. The other half is constantly looking at risk minimization, and constantly seeing what can go wrong. What you are trying to do is optimize risk and minimize risk.

Peter Drucker said it best: entrepreneurs are not risk takers, they are risk optimizers. So many things can go wrong when starting a new venture. You have to keep in mind what all can go wrong and have multiple plan Bs. If something goes wrong, you have to have backup plans, because a lot of things are going to go wrong along the way, and you don't really have a safety net underneath you.

Q: Have you ever made a mistake or failed at something? How did that change you, how did that change your career, and what did you learn from it?

A: I made a lot of mistakes. I ran a startup that didn't pan out too well. I made a lot of poor decisions — people decisions, and strategy decisions in term of products to start and people to hire. I think the biggest lesson is to realize you are going to make mistakes and try to recognize as quickly as possible when have made an error. Don't feel wedded to your decision; make a change and move on. Any time you have made a hiring mistake, or a strategy mistake or a tactical mistake, there's a tendency to hold on to it too long to see how it works out. Once you've decided it's not going to work, it probably won't, and it's time to move on.

Q: How important are innovation and creativity when launching a biotech startup? Some people say those who are more disruptive to the status quo have more success; does that hold true in this field?

A: It's often true, yes. It depends on where you are in a cycle. You can be too early, or too late. That may be the case if there are large numbers of unanswered questions or if you're unclear what the best technical path is, or if you're so early that there are too many science questions that still need to be developed. You as the entrepreneur could be answering a lot of questions and reducing the risk of someone to come afterward. Often the best time to start is not the first or second round. A great example in the HIV area is IliAD, which turns out to be largest success of whole biotech industry. Their HIV drug was the sixteenth drug developed. But they were able to build on the learning and innovations of everyone else and develop the drug with the best characteristics and greatest success.

Our company pioneered inhaled insulin. It turned out to not be a commercial success. It was a huge development effort, it took fifteen years and $3 billion, and others are coming out with products that built on what we did.

Often it's not the innovator or person pioneering the science but others who build on their shoulders who turn out to be successful.

Q: What is the right balance to strike between education, businesses savvy, and creativity when you are a biotech entrepreneur?

A: I think the key to being a biotech entrepreneur is to have some kind of a science innovation to build a startup around. In the role I've always played, I've never been the one to come up with the innovation. I'm not the scientist, I'm not the great visionary; the role I've always played is the person who coalesces the scientists and builds the team, raises the money, and provides the business focus. So you have to think: what role are you are going to take? If you are likely to be the chief scientific officer or chief scientific founder, most of those people are PhDs, MDs, or on the device side — they have gone through a bioengineering program. You need to be pretty well educated. If you are coming in on the business side, you need to have enough experience and also the credibility to raise large amounts of money, to be able to pull a team together and pull a lot of experts together. This is not an area like the Internet that lends itself to nineteen-year-old college-dropout entrepreneurs. It's an area where you need deep scientific expertise, engineering expertise, or business expertise.

Gina Smith

Smith is an award-winning tech journalist and co-author of the best-selling i Woz, the autobiography of Apple cofounder Steve Wozniak.

Q: What ignited the spark in you to become a tech journalist? What is it about the tech industry specifically that you felt needed to be covered better or differently?

A: Why did I pick tech reporting? I started out covering cops, crime reporting. Right out of college, I was a beat reporter for the *Miami Herald*. One day I had to cover an IBM PC announcement. I got to interview the [computer] engineers. I really, really enjoyed it; it was something no one else on the staff felt comfortable doing: talking about computers and translating engineer lingo into plain English and I really liked that challenge. So I asked if I could keep covering it. I had a boss there who was a mentor, and he said the only way to get ahead in journalism was to pick something that few people want to write about — areas where you can really master it. He suggested biotech or computers, and I choose computers.

It was a good decision, because I was one of the first tech reports at *PC Week*. I was right there at the beginning, so a lot of the people who I covered back then are really rich. Like Eric Schmidt, who is now the head of Google, is the guy I used to take out and interview all the time when he was in his twenties. So that was cool, to watch the industry take off, and write the history books.

Q: Tell me how your career began, and how you ended up covering tech and computers for ABC News, and appearing regularly on *Good Morning America*, *World News Tonight*, and 20/20, and also your experience helping to launch Wired and CNET?

A: I wrote about tech for *PC Magazine* and *PC Week*. That was before I ever went to ABC News. I was contacted by this guy — he was a young investment banker who had lost his job, and had come to California because he had an idea. He was starting a publishing network that could compete with Ziff Davis, which was the company that ran *PC Magazine* and *PC Week*, all the computer magazines back then. Everyone thought he was crazy because he didn't know anything about computers, yet he thought he could create a billion-dollar company like Ziff Davis. But I believed him. He and I and John Dvorak and some other computer people in Silicon Valley all sat down and founded CNET. The original idea was not to do a website; it was to do a television network. It was supposed to be the Computer Network. That didn't work out; they couldn't raise any money for that, and I couldn't help them. So they just decided: we'll do a website, and that ended up being what we did.

Q: You are also the author of the *New York Times* bestselling biography on Apple founder Steve Wozniak, *iWoz*. What was that experience like, and what did you learn from working on that project?

A: I had a friend who always went to concerts, who didn't work in computer industry, and she didn't know anyone's name. She sat next to Steve Wozniak and his buddies at Shoreline Amphitheater in California, and they were all wearing these weird fake teeth that lit up, so when the theater got dark, they would smile and they would look like weird Cheshire cats because their mouths were glowing. She thought this was so cool, and she asked, "Who are you?" And he said "Steve Wozniak." She had no idea who he was, but she thought he might be important, so she texted me: "Hey, have you ever heard of Steve Waznak?" I said, "You mean Steve Wozniak?" And she said, "Yeah, that's it!" I said, "Oh my god, I'd love to interview him!" He was already out of computers by the time I started. I'd met Steve Jobs a million times, but never Steve Wozniak. So I had coffee with him, and we were talking about some of these great physics books that were out. There was a physicist who wrote these great books that were fun and light, but still about physics. And Steve was saying how much he liked that guy. And I said, books are great, why don't we do a book that's just like that, but about you, and how you came up with the first true consumer computer?

We met twice a week for a year and a half. I would just turn on my tape recorder and listen to him talk. The thing about Steve is he is so smart, but his mind moves so quickly he never stays on topic, he just keeps bouncing from this to that. And one of the things I learned from that is how to really listen, because a lot of people tried to do books with him before, but got really frustrated because they would ask a question like "What did you and Steve Jobs do on this day?" And he'd start; then he'd change the subject. People got frustrated and they were never able finished the book. So I'd roll the tape and he'd bounce around and it'd be okay. We'd sit in the barbeque pit at the park where he likes to go. Eventually, after six months of interviews, I could listen to them all and start to piece together what actually happened. That was an important lesson.

When we published the book finally, the big problem was the book publisher didn't really put the effort into promoting him. Like really putting him on talk shows. Maybe they would focus on him for a couple weeks, and then they were on to the next book. I really wanted people to remember him, so I helped him get on *Dancing with the Stars*. Because I thought he'd be a terrible dancer, but he'd be funny, and he would definitely get some attention. And that's what kicked off the attention around Steve Wozniak.

Q: If you had the chance to start your career over again, what would you do differently?

A: I would have taken stock options instead of money. When first started CNET, and they finally had a little bit of money, they offered all of us working on it either $5,000 or 5,000 shares of stock. All of us were saying, "I don't know if this company is going to make it." And $5,000 is a lot of money — it was a ton of money at the time. We all took the money, but the stock option would have been worth like a billion dollars right now.

Also, I would have taken even more risks. I always took risks, but I would have taken even more. When the risk profile is high, you should try everything. Take lots of risks and place lots of bets. I wish I would have done that even more at the time.

Q: What are some of the biggest mistakes you've made? How did you recover and how was that reflected in your career?

A: There have been so many mistakes, but as they say, "The more mistakes, the more successes."

What comes to mind is that in 2011 I was hired to relaunch a famous old computer magazine called *Byte*. I was so psyched about this. We were going to do a web version of an amazingly famous computer magazine. They hired me, and they were like, "Yeah, do it." But the idea I had in my head was different from what they really wanted. I went out and hired seventy people. I couldn't pay them yet, but I got seventy people who were into this. We were so in love with this project and created this thing.

Then, as it turned out, they really just wanted a blog to drive traffic to their other websites. Their vision wasn't my vision. My vision was like: "Wow, the Beatles are getting back together." But they were like: "We don't need you to create a multi-million property."

I was really crushed. I ended up quitting in a big huff. They wanted me to cut the staff of seventy, who were basically working for free. They didn't want it to be that popular. They felt like this thing was going crazy. It was messing up the way advertising would slide to their other properties.

We could all see what an amazing property this could be. But to be fair, they didn't want it. I fought them and fought them. So when I left, I'm just hanging around the house. And all these people I had hired started calling me and saying, "We want to come with you!" There were about sixty-two people, and I couldn't take them.

Q: Do you believe there is some sort of pattern or formula to becoming a successful tech entrepreneur?

A: As an entrepreneur, you have to be comfortable with uncertainty and lots of change. Just like the CNET story — we thought it was going to be the Computer Network, and then it became very apparent that was way too expensive, and maybe it's better to do it as a website. We were able to move and turn on a dime. That's one of the many formulas to being a successful entrepreneur, and also knowing if you don't have it in you.

I've been at startups where people were like: "This is too scary. We almost got the money yesterday; we thought we had an investor. And today we don't have anything." It's not for everybody. You have to have it in your blood — an appetite for risk.

Sanjay Parthasarathy

Parthasarathy is a technology expert and former executive at Microsoft. He is the CEO of Indix.

Q: You helped launch .NET at Microsoft. How did the idea for .NET come about?

A: The idea for .NET in part came about through the realization that the programming models on the Internet needed much more loosely coupled architectures, rather than the tightly coupled client-server architectures that were predominate at that time. The loosely coupled architectures at that time were based on what's called web services, which are much more common now. It was a philosophical debate at that point. Ultimately, (MS) management went with loosely coupled architectures. There is a Harvard business case on this topic for further info.

Q: You directed Bill Gates' first trip to India in 1997, which led to a significant investment from Microsoft in the country, and also benefited the growing software industry there. How has that that helped expand Microsoft's software?

A: I went to India in 1996, and I saw it was ready to move into a software space. At MIT I wrote an op-ed piece about how India could be a software superpower, and that was in 1989. I realized this was an opportunity — Bill going there; he had never been there. And this was an opportunity to make a couple points: that there was a market for Microsoft software outside of Europe and the US and Japan and Bill got to see that. But even more importantly, Microsoft has always been a platform company, and developers on platform have always been super important. Having Bill there, he got it, he got the energy and enthusiasm, and a direct result of that was heading up a software-development center. So both at the market and supply level, as part of the supply chain for software, I think the bells went off. It was the right timing. When 1997 happened, there was an incredible amount of interest, and every politician was talking about this in their speeches. Then the year 2000 bug was on the horizon, and people realized the only way to deal with it was to have a software company help them out. It was a good storm, if you will.

Q: Why did you create Indix?

A: After I retired from Microsoft in 2009, I moved my family over to Chennai (India). After twenty-two years away, I couldn't find anything. I grew up in Chennai, but here I was trying to find a place to get furniture, and Google didn't help that much. The way Google works, it prioritizes documents from outside of India, mostly in United States or the UK. Looking at how search engines should work outside the US or UK, that was the first step for the Indix idea to grow from.

Q: What would you say are the five key elements for starting and running a successful business?

A: 1. You need an idea, or a point of view.

2. You need to be able to deal with rejection and failure, because that will happen at some point in time.

3. You need to have an ego, but keep it aside, because even if you have the perfect idea, you have to be able to listen to people.

4. You have to build a team, because without the team, you won't get there alone.

5. You have to be out there to create your own luck. If you're not out there, then good things won't happen.

Q: What top two pieces of advice would you give to college students, or any aspiring entrepreneur, to help you prepare for a career as an entrepreneur?

A: First of all, there is less risk when you are starting out in your career. So the sooner you take the risk, the better. Because along with risk comes learning. Now, I understand a lot of kids graduate college and have a huge financial debt, and they aren't able to take that risk. That's fine. An individual is the best judge of how much risk they are willing to take, and their personal situation. But if you have the opportunity to take risk, the sooner you take it, the better.

Second piece of advice: Most college kids understand the concept that failure is important, that learning from failure is important, but it is really hard to do. It is really hard to take rejection. It's really hard to fail and then wonder what to do with that failure. One of the most important things about failure is to have people who have been through it, and who can mentor others through failure. It's easy enough to say "failure is a stepping stone." Everyone knows how bad it feels, but it really helps to have a mentor, someone to help you along, who has "been there, done that." So finding good mentors is very critical.

Q: If you had the chance to start your career over again, what would you do differently?

A: I might have joined Microsoft a couple years earlier. But the outline of what I would have done would probably be the same. I ended up doing two master's degrees because I didn't know what the hell I wanted to do. I wish I had been a little more mature, and had taken the jump a couple years earlier.

Q: Did you ever make a big mistake and, if so, how did you recover from it?

A: My second job (at Microsoft) was to build a version of Windows that would be an operating system for the television. It was actually built into a CD player/DVD player–looking thing. This was in 1992. I think that may have been a big mistake. But I didn't want to stop there, and I started investigating other approaches. I ended up writing a memo called "Cable Modems Are the Future," which ended up catching Bill's and Paul Allen's attention. My learning from this was: CD-ROMs or DVDs connected to the TV wouldn't give the experience that people are looking for. So that was a mistake, but I was fortunate enough to run into cable modems in a very early demo, so latching on to that was a good thing. And of course cable modems came into their own ten to fifteen years later. So you move on — that is the best way to deal with failure.

Q: Did mentors play a role in your success?

A: Absolutely. I was one of the early Indians at MS. There were a couple of others (from India) who were there much earlier. On the business side, there was a guy who had been there a little longer than me, who eventually ended up mentoring me and the current CEO of Microsoft and a couple others. We learned a lot from him. We learned we could end up being influential and becoming senior at a company where there was no precedent of this. And one of us ended up becoming CEO of Microsoft, so I think he was a good mentor.

Q: Do you believe there is some sort of pattern or formula to becoming a successful entrepreneur?

A: I don't think there is a set rule. Even if you have all the skill and the talent, you have to be out there, you have to have the timing and the luck. You have to let the universe help you. But sometimes you're just not in the right place at the right time. You can do everything right, but the timing may not be OK. That is unfortunate, but it does happen.

Laura Huang

Laura Huang is an assistant professor of management and entrepreneurship at the Wharton School, University of Pennsylvania.

Q: Your field of research examines early-stage investment decisions, and how perceptions influence an individual's ability to make important, high-stakes decisions. Can we better understand what makes entrepreneurs and business leaders successful if we understand how their mind and behavior are linked?

A: Absolutely. I think that it is important to understand how people's thoughts, feelings, and experiences are linked to their subsequent behavior. It's also important to realize how much of an impact our interpersonal relationships have on our perceptions and the attributions we make — which also affect our subsequent behavior. Entrepreneurs, and the customers, suppliers, and investors they interact with, all have their own mental schemas and prototypes that they operate under. It's extremely complex, and that's why it's so hard to predict the judgments and decisions people will make.

Q: What are the most common mistakes that MBAs make when launching startups?

A: There are also a lot of early mistakes that people make, not just MBAs, that end up biting them later on. Founder equity splits…that's one thing to be really careful with, and it's a real art. Also, how you pivot and iterate on your business model. And — of course I'm being overly simplistic here, but in general — the biggest mistake anyone can make with a startup is running out of cash. Never, ever run out of cash.

Q: When would you say is a good time to start your own business? Are there benchmarks you should consider before launching a startup?

A: If you've got a great idea and you've got some initial traction, and your personal circumstances and responsibilities allow for it, I think it's a great time.

Q: How does an aspiring entrepreneur get beyond their fear of starting their own venture? When should you listen to your fear?

A: I'm more concerned with those that don't have fear. I think having fear means that you are taking it seriously and that you are thinking about the decision realistically. It has never been about taking risk, to me. It is about using your fear and letting the risk drive you to come up with solutions that tell you to leap in and go for it, despite that fear. Because you feel so compelled to deliver your product or service, and you are so driven by that…rather than driven by profit, I should add.

Q: What if the thing you're passionate about is already being done?

A: It can always be done differently, or you can always find a way to work with what is currently being done. It's not always about competition; it's also about complementarities and things that are in the same realm.

Q: Would you advise an entrepreneur to stop their venture if it doesn't seem to be working?

A: Yes, if your venture is not working and you are convinced that it is not going to work, I would absolutely advise someone to just liquidate and close. There are too many other things you could be doing. Don't fall prey to "sunk costs" or an "escalation of commitment" type of mentality. If you love the "get your hands dirty" part of entrepreneurship and your venture is not working, but you already have another idea you'd like to pursue, just start your next startup. Or do something else that you've been meaning to do. Whatever you do, it's not going to be fun all the time, but my sense is that you always have a feeling when it's time to just call it quits. There's no shame in that.

Q: Is there a way to judge whether something will really work?

A: I wish there was! If I had a tried-and-true formula, then I would be much richer woman.

ACKNOWLEDGMENTS

To my mom, dad, and grandfather, who have blessed me in every area of my life.

To everyone who graciously provided invaluable insight by allowing me to interview them.

To my editor, Debra Englander, for her never-ending enthusiastic support and invaluable advice.

To the teachers at Stratford Academy who have honed my critical-thinking skills at every level.

To my high school English teachers, Dr. Katz, Mrs. Gumbart, and Mrs. Fleming. Thank you all sincerely for giving me confidence in my writing.

And finally, a large thank you to the amazing team at Post Hill Press, who took a chance on publishing a sixteen-year-old.

ABOUT THE AUTHOR

Deep Patel is a young writer and entrepreneur. He has served as script editor and creative consultant for the comedy *She Wants Me* (2012), produced by Charlie Sheen. Deep has also been featured in *Forbes* and the *Huffington Post*. He is currently finishing up his second book, *The Gray Veil*.

When not writing, Deep is finding a way to give back. He is passionate about children's literacy and plays a vital role in The Mentors Project, which has received recognition from the governor of Georgia for advocating literacy and tutoring underprivileged children.